MANAGING CORPORATE COMMUNICATIONS IN THE AGE OF RESTRUCTURING, CRISIS, AND LITIGATION

Revisiting Groupthink in the Boardroom

DAVID SILVER, APR

J.ROSS PUBLISHING

Copyright © 2014 by J. Ross Publishing

ISBN-13: 978-1-932159-88-2

Printed and bound in the U.S.A. Printed on acid-free paper.

10 9 8 7 6 5 4 3 2 1

Library of Congress Cataloging-in-Publication Data

Silver, David, 1954–
    Managing corporate communications in the age of restructuring, crisis, and
litigation : revisiting groupthink in the boardroom / by David Silver.
        p. cm
    Includes bibliographical references and index.
    ISBN 978-1-932159-88-2 (hardcover : alk. paper) 1. Crisis management.
2. Corporations—Public relations. 3. Corporate image. I. Title.
    HD49.S573 2013
    658.4′5—dc23
                            2013033271

    Direct all inquiries to J. Ross Publishing, Inc., 300 S. Pine Island Rd., Suite
305, Plantation, FL 33324.

Phone: (954) 727-9333
Fax: (561) 892-0700
Web: www.jrosspub.com

Dedication

This book is dedicated to my late mother, affectionately known as Bubba to my children, who encouraged me from a young age to read wide and deep, to write with passion, and to think critically about issues. Her amazing voice still resonates with me today.

Contents

Acknowledgments

In my five-and-a-half year journey to write this book, there have been a number of academic and professional colleagues who have guided me along the way. The journey actually started over three decades ago when I was a freshman at the University of California, Los Angeles (UCLA). In the academic arena, many of my professors nurtured and tutored me how to think critically, read deep and wide, and write with passion and conviction. I studied history as an undergraduate with world-class faculty and loved it so much that I was accepted into the Ph.D. program in History at UCLA. Professors David Myers and Gary Nash were instrumental in teaching me how to think critically about issues and instilled the love history in me, while also guiding me in my academic research. I also want to thank Donna Gulnac, the Director of Access and Information Services at the library at the UCLA School of Law, who gave me unlimited access to conduct research for two years while I was working on my book.

At the University of Southern California (USC) in the Annenberg School of Communication and Journalism, where I was a graduate student, Professor A.J. Langguth, a distinguished former New York Times journalist and author of numerous books, was critical in teaching me how to focus on long-form nonfiction writing at an advanced level. His guidance was crucial when I received my book contract because he offered guidelines on how to write this type of book.

Professor Felix Gutierrez was instrumental in teaching me how to think critically about communications in my research papers and in our many discussions. Professor Jerry Swerling is the Director of the USC Annenberg Strategic Communication and Public Relations Center, where the mission is to advance the study, practice, and value of public relations by means of practical, applied research. The Center's best known project is the biennial Communication and Public Relations Generally Accepted Practices (GAP) study, which is widely recognized as an important source of management-related information for the profession. He was an early supporter of my book and was gracious enough to allow my publisher to include the latest GAP VII study.

At Claremont Graduate University, where I studied at the Peter F. Drucker and Masatoshi Ito Graduate School of Management in the Executive MBA program, Professor Jean Lipman-Blumen's class on crisis management was important for me in finding the central thesis of my book. This Harvard-educated professor introduced the class to Irving Janis's book *Groupthink*, which was brilliant and thought provoking. I used his sociological analysis of groupthink in policy public and government decision making and incorporated this line of reasoning into my argument of how groupthink pervades the boardrooms of corporations worldwide. When I told her that I wanted to use this structure for my book, she encouraged me to pursue this line of reasoning and analysis and I am forever grateful for her guidance and wisdom.

In the professional arena, Julie Green, an editor at the Los Angeles Times, was instrumental in helping me sharpen my writing for the stories that I pitched and eventually wrote for her at the Times. After working as a reporter and editor, the dean of public relations in Los Angeles, Carl Terzian, recruited me to work at his busy firm as an account executive. He mentored me in the business of public relations and taught me the value of client relations in the years I worked for him. In 1994, when I told him I was opening my own public relations firm to focus on financial, crisis, and litigation public relations, he gave me his blessing.

During the five-and-a-half years that I worked on the book while running my firm, my family was a constant source of support. During this period, I watched my three great children—Ira, Alicia and Rachel—grow up from being teens to young adults. I am a lucky father to have such loving and devoted kids.

My wife Michelle, who I always have said is a lot smarter than I, provided guidance and kept me grounded when I got too wrapped up in my book. The love of my life, I am a very lucky man that she agreed to marry me 28 years ago.

Finally, to my wonderful in-laws, Collie and Dianne Wainer, who allowed me to come to their home and work on my book many nights over the preceding years when I needed time to reflect and think.

Biography

Photo credit: Le Staiman

David Silver, APR, is the chief executive officer of Silver Public Relations, a financial public relations firm in Los Angeles that focuses on crisis, litigation, and restructuring financial public relations for publicly traded companies and private corporations. He has counseled more than 1,000 national and global corporations and their boardroom executives in his 25 years as a financial public relations executive.

His proprietary crisis and litigation communications audits are sought out by corporations, as he focuses on the causes and effects of corporate crises. He has written for a number of newspapers—including the *Los Angeles Times*, the *Los Angeles Herald Examiner*, and the *Daily Journal*—has been profiled in the "Leaders and Success" page of *Investor's Business Daily*, and has been interviewed by CBS national news and other network news media as a crisis and litigation public relations expert.

A well-known speaker on the topics of mergers and acquisitions and crisis and litigation public relations, Silver was the only public relations executive to be accredited by the State Bar of California to teach the class, "Managing the Litigation PR Process: When Public Opinion Matters," for hundreds of lawyers and general counsel for corporations in California from 2005–2011. He was the 2009 chair of the Executive Committee for the Financial Communications Section of the Public Relations Society of America (PRSA) and has earned the prestigious APR accreditation from PRSA.

Silver has published numerous articles, in a number of different industry magazines and newspapers, and has spoken to corporate executives around the world on communicating during a crisis. He was also a contributor to *New Investor Relations: Expert Perspectives on the State of the Art.*

Introduction

GROUPTHINK REVISITED

There is a contagion affecting corporations and Wall Street companies doing business in the global marketplace that is destroying reputations and hurting sales. Companies as stellar as Toyota, BP, and Goldman Sachs, who have been the envy of their competitors for decades, are still recovering from periods of extended crises—with senior executives having been fired, products recalled, and regulators summoned to investigate irregularities reported by the *Wall Street Journal*, *CNBC*, *New York Times*, *Financial Times*, and others. When crises boil over to an out-of-control level, the likes of which these companies each experienced, it spreads from the business sector into politics, as elected officials in Congress are pressured by constituents to investigate. The problem: unresponsive boards of directors and senior management at top corporations refuse to explain problems within their companies, giving media outlets free reign to create their own interpretation of stories, which run the crisis gauntlet from oil drilling explosions to malfunctioning automobiles, potentially killing consumers, to shadowy stock deals that border on illegal. Groupthink has set in, and with it, crises are unfolding like raging forest fires that threaten to engulf products, services, careers, and reputations that have, in some cases, been built over centuries.

A BRIEF HISTORY OF GROUPTHINK

The term groupthink was first used by American sociologist, William H. Whyte, in a 1952 *Fortune Magazine* article. In crafting the term, Whyte wrote:

> Groupthink being coinage and admittedly a loaded one, a working definition is in order. We are not talking about the mere instinctive conformity—it is, after all, a perennial failing of mankind. What we are talking about is a rationalized conformity, an open articulate philosophy which holds that group values are not expedient, but right and good as well.

But it was in 1972, in a small but influential book, *Victims of Groupthink*, by Yale University social scientist Irving L. Janis that the term really came to life. Janis explained how a group of highly intelligent people working together to solve a problem can sometimes arrive at the worst possible answer. He called his radical new theory "groupthink" and stated that this line of thinking definitely introduced a new perspective on decision making. He updated and expanded the book in 1982, entitling it *Groupthink: Psychological Studies of Policy Decisions and Fiascos*.

Janis did not write about corporate disasters; rather, in a meticulously researched book, he discussed the Bay of Pigs fiasco as a premier example of groupthink. You might remember journalist and author David Halberstam's characterization of President John F. Kennedy's brilliant group of advisors. Halberstam chronicled how "the best and the brightest" were led astray by a CIA plan for Cuban exiles in Miami to invade Cuba and overthrow Fidel Castro's regime. Kennedy and his executives said that the new president failed to see the futility of this plan because the "bunker mentality groupthink" had already set in; the result was a massive failure for the new president. Janis concentrated on this bunker mentality and concluded that some kind of "psychological contagion, similar to social conformity phenomena observed in studies of small groups, had interfered with their mental alertness." Janis said that this "psychological contagion" had caused the deterioration of mental efficiency, reality testing, and even moral judgment. In-group pressures were the culprits, which had resulted in terrible errors in decision making, which increased the likelihood of a poor outcome. "The more amiability and *esprit de corps* among the members of a policy-making in-group, the greater the danger that independent critical thinking will be replaced by groupthink, which is likely to result in irrational and dehumanizing actions directed against out-groups," Janis said.

In regards to Kennedy and the Bay of Pigs, the *esprit de corps* among Kennedy's advisors could be simply summarized as an understanding among the group that, after being humiliated by Khrushchev less than a year prior in Vienna, the young president wanted to show his manhood by making his mark. So there you had a room full of Harvard graduates and executive whiz kids left to make something of Eisenhower's funding during his administration, Cuban ex-patriots looking to reclaim their country from Castro, and a president with something to prove. When it came time to decide whether to give the order to overthrow, history suggests that the private consensus was that it was a bad idea, but no one in the group wanted to speak up and be seen as a deviant. No one wanted to let the president down. They saw how much Kennedy wanted to move forward and they let him go ahead—head first into a major fiasco.

Janis's analysis raised a number of fundamental questions about when group processes interfere with effective decision making. The danger arises when conditions foster shared illusions, resulting in misjudgments. Janis primarily wished to increase awareness about the importance of emotion and personality dynamics, so that—psychologically—group dynamics are taken into conscious consideration. This should be a part of the understanding of any collective action.

Janis's case studies of major fiascos in the public policy arena show how groupthink can result in "an appalling comedy of errors that ends up as a tragedy." Participants "adhered to group norms and pressures toward uniformity, even when their policy was working badly and had unintended consequences that disturbed the conscience of its members," he wrote. "Members consider loyalty to the group the highest form of morality." Those participating in critical decisions, Janis found, had failed to consider the full range of alternatives, or to consult experts who could offer different perspectives. The "group" rejected outside information and opinion unless "it supported their preferred policy." Janis also offered solutions for preventing groupthink.

His seminal book is still studied in colleges, business schools, management training seminars, and academia. In fact, in 2005, the presidential commission on U.S. intelligence, examining the question of weapons of mass destruction, released a lengthy study about "'groupthink' on an international scale." They specifically identified groupthink as a reason Western intelligence services decided Iraq posed a genuine weapons-of-mass-destruction threat, when in fact that was very much in question. One senator involved in the authorization vote to go to war cited groupthink as well. Lincoln Chafee was one of only seven senators to break with his party and vote against the war. Ten years later, as the Governor of Rhode Island, Chafee looked back and reflected on the atmosphere at the time of the vote. "You would think after Vietnam, people would be hesitant, but it happened. Any time you get these emotions of fear and anger, it's always possible. It's groupthink."

CORPORATE GROUPTHINK

I thoroughly believe that the arguments Janis made about public policy fiascos can and should be applied to corporate America—in particular, to corporate problems with communication. In my observations, C-Suite executives use the "groupthink" methodology when confronted with a crisis. Just as countries suffer terrible crises from which it is hard to recover, so do corporations—no matter how seemingly large and powerful they may be. When target audiences turn against a company's executives, products, or services, the effects can be devastating. Mistakes resulting from a faulty communications model can destroy a company, its reputation, and eventually, its revenues and profits.

With this in mind, I propose a slightly modified definition of groupthink: the state of paralysis that takes over a corporate boardroom or business unit and is most devastating when a company is faced with a crisis, restructuring, or litigation. The conditions Janis detailed are a threat to innovation and are potentially fatal when media scrutiny is applied. Jeff Bezos, founder and CEO of Amazon, sees groupthink as the enemy of independent ideas and has gone to great lengths to keep it from spreading—actively favoring decentralization and disorganization as its natural obstacles. Bezos has linked the size of a working group to how vulnerable it is to groupthink behavior, instituting a rule that any team that could not be fed with two pizzas is too large. When, at a corporate retreat, several managers advocated increased communication between employees, Bezos shot the idea down, declaring, "communication is terrible."

If communication is terrible at your company, than groupthink is inevitable. Containment and other workarounds might make for short-term solutions, but they fail to deal with the root of the problem. It isn't communication that causes groupthink;

it's unskilled and poor communication that creates the conditions in which valid ideas are stifled, and misjudgment becomes the norm. Ultimately, my intention with this book is to argue that communication skills must be valued, improved, and embraced to create a corporate culture with greater immunity to the effects of groupthink.

In the first part of the book, we will review the case studies of several companies whose failure to communicate effectively paved the way for disaster. Along the way, we will look at the theories of communication that determine success or failure, and lay the groundwork for a successful alternative in terms of organizational hierarchy. At the conclusion of Part I, we will look at Steve Jobs's tenure at Apple as the corporate communications role model to be emulated, highlighting other companies that used their ability to communicate successfully to navigate through potential crises.

In Part II, we will create our own crisis and follow it through an organization of our own making, unprepared to deal with it and destined to be on the wrong end of the news cycle. From here, we will begin the process of remaking corporate America, examining tools—such as the communications audit and big picture factors, related to business education and hiring priorities—before finally putting our ideas into action.

In the end, it is my objective to make the following arguments:

- Groupthink is a real threat to the sustainability of companies at every level of business, magnified by the communication advances of the twenty-first century.
- The spectacular meltdowns we've all read about, followed on the news, or commented on in our social media feeds were all completely avoidable.

- The reason these crises spun out of control was a failure of communication.
- The deficient communication skills within a company are a near-systemic failure of business and education.
- There is a solution, which uses continuing education and reprioritizing values in hiring decisions.
- Finally, not only can communication effectively neutralize groupthink but also, when valued and properly utilized by an organization facing potential distress, it is the single most important tool in controlling the message to better pave the way for a positive outcome. Business and law schools should take some of the blame for not teaching communications as an important core course to the future boardroom executives and legal counsels of the world.

At J. Ross Publishing we are committed to providing today's professional with practical, hands-on tools that enhance the learning experience and give readers an opportunity to apply what they have learned. That is why we offer free ancillary materials available for download on this book and all participating Web Added Value™ publications. These online resources may include interactive versions of material that appears in the book or supplemental templates, worksheets, models, plans, case studies, proposals, spreadsheets and assessment tools, among other things. Whenever you see the WAV™ symbol in any of our publications, it means bonus materials accompany the book and are available from the Web Added Value Download Resource Center at www.jrosspub.com.

Downloads for *Managing Corporate Communications in the Age of Restructuring, Crisis, and Litigation* include GAP VII: The Seventh Communication and Public Relations Generally Accepted Practices Study from the USC Annenberg School for Communication and Journalism, a checklist for performing an internal communications audit, and a presentation on effectively communicating during a litigation.

Part I

Case Studies

1

Managing Reputation in Distressed Markets

It was Ken Chenault, CEO of American Express, who may have summed it up best. In an interview for *Fortune Magazine* a few years ago, he said, "We have to remember that reputations are won or lost in a crisis." There should have been a million great reputations won over the last decade. From Chenault's premise, it was clear that managing corporate communications in distressed markets was a far more important skill than managing corporate communications in rising and stable markets.

Since World War II, CEOs and senior managers were lionized for providing the engine of growth and success to American corporations. No longer is this the case. The image has been shattered—perhaps beyond repair. In the 1950s and early '60s, CEOs were the "rock stars" of their day. Now, CEOs are suspected of having nearly brought down the entire financial system, and actual rock stars have greater credibility. The public has been watching a steady stream of well-known executives either being led out of their absurdly luxurious offices in handcuffs or fleeing the wreckage of their posts on golden parachutes. That sense of trust and integrity, which had permeated much of corporate America's boardrooms, is gone and has been replaced with something corrosive. Groupthink, all too often, has become the only method of defense corporations know how to use in the court of public opinion. And groupthink is a hard sell, even for an accomplished communicator. People sense the arguments are fatally flawed.

Perhaps it is not accidental that common knowledge says the value of a CEO's good reputation has been downgraded. This is so despite Ernst & Young's recent study measuring how much a firm's reputation depended on the reputation of its CEO: a full third of the respondents said the reputation of senior management was almost as important as hard financial data in deciding whether to do business with a firm.

However, now that there are more restructuring and litigation crises going on, this will begin to change. A good reputation will help even more in the competition for capital and customers. Reputation management is an important part of the task of managing communications strategically. So, where can corporate executives go to find out what are the most common mistakes in formulating this strategy? Hopefully, this book can be one useful resource.

Corporations nowadays have to learn to adapt to increasingly volatile global business environments—environments that are far more complex and litigious than ever before. Communication must be more diverse as well as more segmented. It's a serious paradox that even communication experts have trouble wrapping their minds around. It was much simpler back in the old days of "mass media." Mass media is still a player, but it is no longer the only player.

4

Adding to this is the current revival of mergers and acquisitions in the marketplace. With all the corporations that are getting in trouble, the bigger fish are circling the littler fish. Sometimes they are "friendly," but they often make such pretense, only to bide their time. There are also a slew of crises on the business landscape—with lawsuits, restructurings, and layoffs that can hit any company at any time in its business cycle.

CRISIS AT TOYOTA

In 2010, the world's leading automaker, Toyota Motor Corporation, started a massive recall and halted production of a number of models in response to accusations of gas pedals getting stuck, causing runaway acceleration. The problem had been reported more than a decade before, in 1999, but the Japanese company failed to respond immediately to growing public anger and resentment—even after a dramatic and much-publicized recording of a 911 call suggested that the supposed defect was directly responsible for four deaths. When the company did respond, it seemed as if executives were being evasive by blaming their suppliers, resulting in a public relations disaster.

Toyota, which for decades had built a stellar reputation with buyers, started exporting cars to the United States more than 50 years earlier and attained the status of the top automaker in the world, known for technical expertise and reliability. When the U.S. Congress launched an investigation into the reported unwanted acceleration, the three major rental companies in the United States cancelled their Toyota orders—Avis alone removed 20,000 Toyotas from its fleet—and the firm's reputation took an enormous hit. In late January, according to newspaper reports, U.S. Transportation Secretary Ray LaHood ordered

Toyota to stop sales to the public. For months, Toyota maintained that the problem was caused by floor mats trapping the accelerator, and although they maintained that these mats were improperly installed by retailers—a claim that was eventually vindicated—it still led to the company's first major recall of 4.3 million vehicles in 2009. At the beginning of 2010, Toyota recalled an additional 2.3 million vehicles, claiming that certain Toyota models had defective gas pedal mechanisms. In an interview in the *Los Angeles Times* on January 28, 2010, Jeremy Anwyl, the chief executive of Edmunds.com, the authority on the car industry, said, "The real question is how Toyota moves forward. There are still a lot of questions that Toyota has not provided answers to."

Toyota not only lost millions in sales but also, and more importantly, it lost credibility and trust in the global marketplace because it did not communicate effectively with the public immediately from the advent of the crisis. With the avalanche of negative press, new problems emerged. By February of 2010, the problem of sticky accelerator pedals had moved into federal courts, with a number of class action lawsuits being filed in federal courts in Los Angeles.

The Daily Journal, the largest legal newspaper in the country, also reported that the automaker spent much of the previous year battling an attack from a disgruntled former in-house counselor, who accused the company of repeated discovery violations in rollover lawsuits. In Japan, executives were concerned about the threat of a U.S. probe into the possibility of electromagnetic interference with the electronic throttle systems. In addition, there were complaints that the Prius was having brake problems. And, when some senior Toyota officials refused to acknowledge the problems with some of its models, the company's problems snowballed into an avalanche. The National Highway Traffic

Safety Administration joined the investigation, and the excellent reputation the company had worked hard to build in the United States marketplace for more than 50 years started to crumble. Toyota had built up a huge reservoir of goodwill decades before, by building factories in the United States and hiring a substantial number of American workers—creating about 175,000 new jobs. But that goodwill seemed to be unraveling in a wave of distressing news, affecting its image, sales, employee morale, and the bottom line.

Akio Toyoda, grandson of the founder of Toyota, Kiichiro Toyoda, took over as president of the company in mid-2009. It is not easy to know his state of mind, of course, but—by saying almost nothing publicly on the occasion of the first recall, and then issuing only a cursory statement on the occasion of the second recall—he failed to bolster public confidence. Rather, quite the opposite occurred. Public opinion rapidly turned against the automaker in the beginning of 2010. As he was attending the global meeting of financial and industrial leaders in Davos, Switzerland, it was clear that a problem of major proportions was swirling around him, with the global financial media hounding him for an explanation to the problems with the cars.

A series of half measures didn't help matters. One of these was a letter in major newspapers from Jim Lentz, president of Toyota's U.S. division. Lentz also appeared on NBC's *Today* show. But it was all to no avail. From the *Wall Street Journal* to the *New York Times*, from *the Los Angeles Times* to the *Washington Post*, Toyota was taking a pounding. Other major publications—including *USA Today*, the *Financial Times*, *BusinessWeek*, *Forbes*, *Fortune*, and *Barron's*—as well as financial television shows on CNBC and national radio talk shows were all painting Toyota in a profoundly negative manner. Elected officials were not far behind, using the opportunity to take to the pulpit and demand investigations, which created an aura of political opportunism.

REPUTATION

The Toyota story is a perfect example of how a failure to communicate initially, when the problem was manageable, created a public relations disaster for a firm that had built up a great deal of goodwill. What makes Toyota's story so appropriate, as both a study of communication failure and a critique of the typical groupthink response by companies wanting to limit participation in their own bad story, is that Toyota was eventually vindicated on the facts.

The probe into Toyota by the National Highway Traffic Safety Administration and NASA found, "There is no electronic-based cause for unintended high-speed acceleration in Toyotas." The report attributed the allegations of runaway vehicles to "pedal misapplication" and concluded, "Toyota vehicles are safe to drive." Toyota was right about their products but wrong in the manner with which it tried to control the message (or refusal to engage the process), and it paid a heavy price for failure.

Reputation is a corporation's number one asset, and the Toyota study shows how a global company can be successful at building a great line of products and a stellar reputation, but have that reputation nearly destroyed, resulting in the loss of hundreds of millions in sales and profits. By not understanding how to communicate in a crisis through the global financial media—the ultimate gatekeeper of reputation in the court of public opinion—a company is stacking the deck against itself.

All organizations, whether corporations or countries, are greater than the sums of their parts. A corporation has incredible reputational powers beyond their products and services, power which is communicated through their workers and executives. This is the source of their strength and can also be the epicenter of their worst crises. Had Toyota leveraged its reputation into targeted communication at the onset of the scandal, they might have gotten through it relatively unscathed. Of course, in hindsight, knowing that Toyota's products weren't to blame gave them the potential to escape unharmed; other companies have found themselves in less fortunate circumstances.

RECOGNIZING THE GROUPTHINK RESPONSE

As the Toyota scandal began to wind down, a new and even bigger story involving a big multinational corporation thrust itself into the headlines. The explosion of the Deepwater Horizon, an offshore oil platform in the Gulf of Mexico immediately caused the deaths of eleven workers, but that tragic loss of life was only the beginning. British Petroleum (BP) owned the Macondo Prospect oil field that Deepwater had been drilling, and the company soon found itself at the center of the largest marine oil spill in recorded history, as millions of gallons of oil and a seemingly never-ending stream of bad news began polluting the Gulf region.

We will discuss the BP disaster in more detail in Chapter 3, but suffice it to say: the fact that two major corporations got into trouble at about the same time was not mere coincidence, as both were victims of groupthink responses. The only antidote to a condition in which good ideas are stifled and poor options are left unchecked by professionals who know better, is effective communication. How a corporation communicates internally and externally will ultimately determine whether it survives or perishes in the court of public opinion—the most important audience an executive or corporation will have. Proper internal communication, engaged by employees who can critically assess a situation and deliver key points up the ladder, is just as essential as the external communication skills of whoever is charged with relaying the message to the public. The amazing thing about groupthink is that its victims include brilliant global executives, who built great brands, but failed miserably to communicate when a crisis hit. Groupthink is not necessarily a disease of incapable people; it is a feeble response from brilliant business and financial executives, who never received the training or learned the skills in business or law school.

Toyota, for instance, spent billions to build a great brand and goodwill in the United States for half a century, but—when it came to the crisis involving the alleged acceleration problems in its cars—they reacted as most corporate executives would, surrendering to the groupthink mentality. They were worse than amateurish; they appeared to be completely untrained for handling the crisis. The same was true for BP in the Gulf. Both companies blamed outside vendors at first, but that did not resonate well with a public fearing for its safety. The companies followed by issuing unconvincing excuses, and compounded their situations by hiding relevant technical issues.

What is it about highly educated successful business executives who act like neophytes when trying to communicate with the outside world in a crisis? Toyota and BP are not the only global corporations that failed to understand the importance of communication in distressed environments. What is odd is that these corporations tend to have seasoned high-level communication executives in-house, charged with developing effective communications strategies in just such distressed environments. But the problem is not in the suites devoted to communicating with the outside world. The problem is in the corporate boardrooms and C-suites in that these executives have not genuinely learned to embrace what their own communications executives are telling them in tough situations.

When you deal in the court of public opinion, which once only meant mainstream media but now includes a vast blogosphere and millions of socially connected users, you have to communicate your message early and frequently. Relaying your carefully constructed narrative spin becomes a delicate tightrope walk, as your story won't be believable if it isn't truthful. It's the old story told by Mark Twain, who said the basic reason he didn't lie was that it was too hard to keep track of them all.

It's good practice to create a storyboard for your corporation with the key components of the narrative in mind. And it's not only good practice but essential that you have the highest ranking executive of the corporation, who can be articulate in telling the story as your company perceives it, communicate with the public. That executive has to tell the story often and must come off as transparent. If the press or the public detects vague or evasive language, designed to hide facts or allow backtracking later on from your official response, they'll pounce.

There is nothing wrong with walking into a press conference, having a strong sense of what the reporters want to know, and answering questions in a satisfying way. You will garner real goodwill if you're sincere, and to be sincere, you have to communicate an attitude of letting the chips fall where they may. Speak honestly about the faults of your company and more importantly, explain your solutions. Don't hide the facts, be forthright and honest, and don't talk in "corporate speak," which is a reputation killer.

If Toyota had called me to ask for my initial ideas to prevent this unfolding groupthink disaster, I would have recommended that Mr. Toyoda himself hold a national press conference in the United States. Doing so right away would have conveyed the notion that Toyoda took the story and the safety implications surrounding it seriously. My advice to Mr. Toyoda would have been to remind the American people, along with the global audience, that Toyota Motors has been part of the American business cycle and numerous communities for more than 50 years, we employ over 175,000 Americans in the United States, and we will address this problem. This approach could have started the process of healing for the victims and given a true explanation to the unfolding disaster.

Had Mr. Toyoda outlined the faults that belonged to Toyota and their solutions to them, and done so often and early, it would have been the start of a successful communication effort. However, corporations are run by human beings, and human beings are prone to failures especially when such a phenomenon as groupthink is pushing them toward it. Groupthink is like a gigantic force of nature: a tsunami tightly drowning the executives in its powerful grasp, and making normally powerful and intelligent executives act in irrational ways.

Having not had a ringside seat for the deliberations inside Toyota which prompted the course of action (or inaction) they embarked upon, I cannot specifically state where the breakdown occurred, only that it very clearly happened. I know this because the Toyota response flies in the face of the fundamentals of effective communication. Whether the rationale for it was not dignifying a bogus accusation, not feeding an unflattering story, or not leaving the company vulnerable to legal response, the only thing Toyota succeeded in doing was not controlling the story. When someone misunderstands you in an unflattering way, you correct them; when the wrong message gets out about your company with the potential for serious damage, you launch a campaign to set the record straight. Considering the stakes, the notion of the public knowing the truth about your company and its product is never "not worth it," especially when there is nothing wrong with the product. What's left is that at some level, highly educated executives allowed themselves either to be talked out of doing the only thing that made sense or they just never considered it. Perhaps there was direct pressure to do so; regardless, groupthink helped it happen. When corporations fail, groupthink is often the root cause because no one dares stand up to say there might be a better way.

SENDING A MESSAGE

Managing corporate communications in distressed markets is tremendously challenging because negative news sells better than positive news. Telling the truth is important. Prevaricating is never a good strategy. If you have to do something to correct a situation, you must tell the truth about it. Truth still sells. Had Toyota not conveyed the perception that they were trying to stall in communicating about their problems, they might have saved themselves additional heartache, and their failure to do so was an open invitation the global financial media took advantage of. This, in turn, negatively impacted Toyota's litigation problems, since a great number of class action lawsuits were filed and needed to be handled. A feeding frenzy of negative media hurt the brand in real ways, despite 50 years of successful business in America. Its greatest loss, of course, was its reputation, badly damaged by a communications error.

All things being equal, a corporation that values and practices the art of communication will weather a crisis better. Having a CEO who understands the importance of communication ensures that the communications process is proactive, so it can cope with turbulent global markets by eliminating as many barriers as possible to getting the message out. There are many times a corporation must take a position in the public marketplace in order to survive. One *New York Times* foreign affairs columnist described this as the "democratization of technology and finance." It is on these terms that corporate communications has to be redefined, and for which more effective models need to be implemented. These new models must be used as a foundation for educating senior management in corporate communications.

When a crisis does hit, the ability of a corporation to get its message out, correctly decoded and ready to translate, is essential. Of course, the message a corporation sends may not survive all the variables: the message may not be understood, it may be altered by biased sources, or it may have missed the point entirely. That is why feedback is necessary. Without feedback, you won't know whether your communication was successful—you won't know if you got through. If your position requires you to get through to an audience, then a muted or non-response is not an option. This is exactly what we saw from Toyota: a quiet response sent against the louder message that theirs was a dangerous product, possibly responsible for the raw fear heard on the 911 calls. Is it any wonder which message the public listened to? By not getting through with the truth, or at least their version of it, people believed the only story they heard, and Toyota paid the price for it.

2

Litigation and the Court of Public Opinion

Twenty-first century corporations are moving targets. The proliferation of litigation has become prevalent as companies try to do business. Sometimes, the only way out of a problem is to file Chapter 11 as different crises surface—using bankruptcy to restructure businesses that have become weak—for one reason or another. Such variables as litigation and financial meltdowns, in both domestic and international markets, are now part of the cost of doing business on a global basis.

On September 15, 2008, the collapse and bankruptcy of Lehman Brothers, the venerable Wall Street firm, triggered a financial free fall in the world economy, leaving in its wake a domino effect, which saw world financial markets teetering on the brink of disaster. A terrible contagion had spread across the globe. In the run up that preceded it, if someone dared to express a negative thought or doubt regarding the resiliency of the United States financial markets, it was quickly buried by all those who were convinced the good times would last forever and that the risk was spread out and diversified. It was as clear an example of communications groupthink as can be imagined. But 2008 was the start of a financial catastrophe, not seen since the Great Depression of the 1930s, and it was global in scale.

During the first decade of the new millennium, CEOs and boards of directors embraced the abundant money provided by lightly regulated financial institutions, believing that they were leveraging their way into the new age. But when all that cheap money started showing up as huge losses on their balance sheets, boardrooms remained silent. The mania that suggested it would be an unlimited resource was suddenly gone. The predominant thinking of all the experts on Wall Street proved to be a mere illusion. That's what invariably happens when groupthink permeates the corporate boardroom.

The collapse of the world financial system also exerted a heavy political toll. As had an earlier president confronted with the collapse of the financial system 80 years before, Barack Obama, the young new president, chose Keynesian solutions. In essence, these solutions meant a leveraging of the future to save the present. It's a technique fraught with dangers and perils, but if done right, it has proven to be the faithful standby governments use to solve problems. At the time, it also appeared to be the only avenue left to stem the substantial losses in wealth that were occurring every day in the financial markets.

Some argued that the "unseen guiding hand" of the marketplace should have been used for a solution instead: Let the chips fall where they may. Let the car companies fail. Let the banks fail. Let businesses fail across the country. But those who believed this failed to make a compelling enough argument, because the danger of the Great Recession becoming the Great Depression was all too real. And most people—on Wall Street and on Main Street—saw the need for some sort of government intervention.

There is no doubt we've been living in distressed and turbulent times, with namesake U.S. companies, like General Motors and Chrysler, going through bankruptcy and restructuring. Additionally, the government needed to step in to get protection from its creditors for Bear Stearns, saving the company by financing a quick sale to JP Morgan. All the while, a multitude of corporations and quasi-governmental entities were trying to negotiate better terms for the high levels of debt they had accumulated in this easy credit free-for-all. It was the same easy credit that everyone thought would last forever. It didn't.

The *laissez-faire* policies, which fueled the decade before the fall, had been forged with good intentions and support from the Federal Reserve and other governmental entities. But mixed in with the best intentions were some of the worst results. Bankers took unnecessary financial risks—betting the house with shareholder monies—and the reputation of American financial institutions, and capitalism itself, suffered tremendously at the global level.

The first decade of the new millennium had been crowded with tales of miraculous financial vehicles being created by "brilliant" executives with extensive resumes. These vehicles had names that showed their sophistication—derivatives, known as credit-default swaps, were tools supposedly intended to limit and spread the risk. They didn't do this, of course. Instead, they helped bring the world economy to its knees. With the collapse of Lehman Brothers—a company founded in 1850, which funded many venerable companies, such as Macy's, Campbell Soup Company, B.F. Goodrich, and American Airlines—corporate executives all over Wall Street ran to their "bunkers" to hide from the financial media. Until that point, the media had

17

lionized many of those same executives as "giants of industry" and the corporations they headed as beacons of light of the great American financial system, an inspiration for the rest of the world. The democratization of finance and technology had allowed financial systems around the world to become interconnected in such a manner that when the collapse started, it created a tsunami effect that still resonates today.

The collapse seemed to signal the end of the American hegemony of Wall Street. Corporations and companies were filing Chapter 11 in such significant numbers, trying to survive the devastation that was hitting the global marketplace, that not only did the US financial system begin to suffer but the financial implosion also created havoc in Europe, Latin America, and parts of Asia. Executives and general counsels from more than one corporate boardroom rushed to defend themselves in the court of law. As they tried to reorganize their companies' secured and unsecured debts, the problems being created in the courts were compounded. The result is that a growing percentage of the core resources—and profits—of corporate America were diverted to the lawyers and more importantly, the court of law, with the court of public opinion being ignored in the process.

Litigation costs are rising so fast in California—it leads the nation—that according to a Litigation Trends Survey from the international law firm Fulbright & Jaworski, almost 91 percent of the state's corporations had lawsuits commenced against them in 2009. Corporations that had more than $1 billion in revenue were, on average, fighting 147 legal cases. This means the cost of doing business has gotten more expensive for everyone—from shareholders to consumers. At the same time, the general public, among others, became much more critical of companies and their corporate executives, who play with the corporate books and do not respond quickly to conditions in the marketplace. The target audience of many large corporations today is also demanding increasing transparency.

FAILING IN THE COURT OF PUBLIC OPINION

With so much attention diverted to historic crises and widespread litigation, the most underlooked weakness of executives in the C-suite and the corporate boardroom—indeed, in the whole Wall Street environment—is their lack of understanding of the court of public opinion. It is no accident that this is where you see the biggest fiascos developing. But, you have to understand the process. When a distressing situation arises which potentially affects the bottom line, executives have to understand how to communicate key messages, both internally and externally. One of the cornerstones of this book, in fact, is an argument about just such situations. For the tendency seems to be: when highly educated executives are facing difficult situations in litigation, bankruptcy, and reorganization, they wither away and are terrified to take any sort of action to confront and explain the negative innuendos and rumors about things that begin appearing in the financial mass media. Yet, it is in just such moments that they most need to communicate with their shareholders, bondholders, customers, vendors, employees, lenders, partners, and regulators.

Corporate executives will spend millions on building a company by recruiting a skilled workforce, expanding products and services in the global economy, raising their stock prices and valuation through proactive marketing of the company's brand, and yet fail miserably in understanding the communication process. They need to break out of groupthink-inspired behavior and develop the most important skill they can possess for doing business in the new global marketplace. Boardroom leaders, more than ever, have to understand the need for communication. They have to learn to think outside of the "groupthink communications" box. They need to stop undervaluing the skills involved in communication and grasp how crucial a good reputation is to successfully grow, and potentially save, a company.

There are usually three scenarios where things can easily go wrong—litigation, restructuring, or crises of one kind or another. Since the new millennium dawned, the world has suddenly changed. Communication has become instant with the Internet; through it, platforms like Twitter, Facebook, as well as mobile applications, have further paved the way for speedy and instant communication. With instant media coverage, instant communication means audiences find out about a corporation's misfortune almost immediately. You can't hide anything from your internal or external audiences.

Public relations and communications have been an integral part of corporate America for the last 100 years. Yet, it is apparent that corporate executives still do not fully understand how powerful communication is in positioning a company's services, products, and executives in the public arena—especially when a corporation is forced to defend its reputation in the court of public opinion. The aftermath of the upheaval in the financial markets will force executives of companies from around the globe to learn how to cope by using strategic communications to defend their companies during times of great duress. And this will also position them to benefit tremendously, as the business environment improves and the economy starts growing again over the next few years.

The main thing required of executives in the C-Suites is to understand that a company's reputation is its number one asset. When executives in the C-suite are hit with a crisis, they traditionally form a "bunker" mentality—a collective state of mind that is synonymous with groupthink. Avoiding the bunker mentality and preventing groupthink from becoming the *modus operandi* is the key to success, as the alternative results in damage to a company's image and identity with all target audiences because the corporation is only communicating its worse self. And that, of course, is a recipe for disaster. As sophisticated and educated as these executives are, their continued regression toward groupthink communications has only served to undermine their reputations. Worse, as the psychological drive for consensus at any cost suppresses disagreement and prevents the appraisal of alternatives, they will be damned to make the same mistakes over and over.

For many executives, what has gone wrong is that they have handled crises in a thoroughly amateurish manner because of their lack of communication skills. Though they may be highly skilled, too often CEOs, CFOs, managing partners, presidents, senior managers, and corporate lawyers are not seasoned in communicating to a mass audience, as many were never taught effective strategies and tactics for doing so in business school. Business schools teach case studies of a company, person, or project over a certain amount of time, looking at the challenges, objectives, and strategies of the firm to figure out what did and did not happen along the way to success or failure. It's a demanding approach. The idea is that the best way for students to become astute businessmen or businesswomen is to learn to make decisions from rigorous knowledge of the specifics in any given situation and to know how to analyze those specifics for the best results.

According to one estimate, during a two-year MBA program, students will prepare and discuss approximately 800 case studies. Business schools also have courses in finance, accounting, IT, sales, management, and legal ethics, to name just a few. Yet the fact is that the number crunchers are traditionally appointed to CEO positions. The real power goes directly to whoever best understands, at least theoretically, a company's balance sheet and income statements. A prerequisite to running a company is dealing with financial statements. This is the "hard core curriculum" for all wishing to climb the corporate ladder to the C-suite.

Do you notice what's missing? Again, communication—if offered in business schools—is shamefully dismissed. When taught, if at all, communication is considered a "soft" or elective discipline. The truth is, of course, that the person with an ability to communicate effectively is much more rare than yet another number cruncher. The argument could be made that communication is a much more valuable skill. Yet business schools are remiss in teaching communication with real seriousness.

This attitude follows executives and lawyers into C-suites and executive boardrooms around the world. Professor Paul Argenti, a leading business scholar of corporate communications from Dartmouth University's Tuck School of Business, agreed that business schools don't take communications as seriously as finance, accounting, and management: "This has been a major problem in business education, communications is not taken seriously in the school curriculum; it is considered soft and it reflects in the poor manner that corporate boardrooms communicate."

"The problem is that corporate communications only becomes extremely important when there is a crisis that will affect a corporation's reputation," Argenti said. "It is such an important function in corporations in communicating a company's message, products, or services, but is not considered seriously." Professor Argenti has spent years on the faculty at Tuck, educating business students and executives on the importance of corporate communications. His current opinion of the state of business communications is, "It has gotten better, but there still needs to be an understanding that corporate communications is a critical function for a company not only to survive, but thrive."

Ironically, business and law school students have traditionally been taught to reason critically before making major decisions—just not in the one area where they really need to be critical thinkers, namely, in communicating with themselves and their external audiences. In Chapter 9, we will look at why the critical skills of the current generation of business and law school graduates seem to be on the decline, and propose a radical shift in thinking that will allow corporations to identify the best assets available to them, in terms of education and background, both with existing staff and potential hires.

THE ROAD TO EFFECTIVE COMMUNICATION

As the media has become much more aggressive, in part because of 24-hour cable news, corporations find themselves constantly pursued for answers, responses, and commentary. This is partly the result of the aftermath of the 1990s, when critics besmirched financial journalists as little more than cheerleaders during the Internet revolution. Similarly, when money began to flow to corporations in the first decade of the millennium, the same journalists were accused of being apologists for cheap money.

What is odd about downplaying communication skills is that in the nation's boardrooms, there really is nothing more basic to success than effective communication: nothing, because the art and science of public relations is at the bottom of every successful business story. Communication is a natural component of human existence, stretching back to the first time one human confronted another. Its importance is vital to the functioning of society and the world. It was about 100 years ago that the importance of communication began to be understood, with the

23

rise of industrialization, the modern corporation, and the management theories of the corporation.

A corporate executive who understands and values the importance of communication will see how it also involves leadership and management functions. These functions are crucial to a company's survival. Business scholars, such as Warren Bennis, a professor at the University of Southern California in the Marshall School of Business and an expert in leadership, have traditionally said that what distinguishes successful leadership is doing the right things and making the correct choices. The late Peter Drucker, a scholar of business management, said that what underlies that skill is, again, doing things right. Thus, corporate executives who understand leadership and management should also understand communications and the role public relations contribute to a company's decision-making process. Effective and truthful communication also makes a CEO look like a leader and thus, must be valued as part of managerial decision making. When a corporation's general counsel insists on a "no comment," it often indicts a company in the court of public opinion—even though thorny legal issues are commonplace for corporations doing business in today's marketplace. Also, the question of corporations "telling the truth" is not an academic one, nor is it just about the deleterious effect being less than truthful can have on a company's management and leadership style.

In 2002, commercial free speech became an issue that rocked corporations nationally when a California Supreme Court ruled in a 4-3 vote that Nike could be sued over its corporate policy statements. The court ruled that corporations could be sued for false advertising in their policy statements when they do so in public relations campaigns. The California Supreme Court ruled that statements made by the Oregon-based shoemaker, denying allegations that some overseas factories were sweatshops, was a form of commercial speech not protected by the first amendment. This is especially important in California, which has tougher consumer protection laws than most states. The justice who wrote the opinion, Joyce Kennard, stated:

> Because in the statements at issue here Nike was acting as a commercial speaker, because its intended audience was primarily the buyers of its products, and because the statements consisted of factual representations about its own business operations, we conclude that the statements were commercial speech for purposes of applying state laws designed to prevent false advertising and other forms of commercial deception.

Nike appealed the ruling to the U.S. Supreme Court, and on June 26, 2003, the court dismissed the appeal and sent the case back to the California Supreme Court. Five U.S. Supreme Court justices rejected the central argument that Nike's speech could be restricted as purely commercial. So, effective communication should be truthful because truthful communication resonates with those who hear it, but also because there can be strong legal reasons for serious candor.

THE MARGIN CALL

With Toyota, we observed a company's failure to take an aggressive stand in defending its reputation against damaging accusations. As Wall Street crumbled, the situational failure of Toyota's executives was a way of life carried on by an entire sector of the global investment economy. The blindness to repercussion was amplified by a resistance toward upsetting the status quo—to shine a rational light on excessive risk would have meant ending the party while the bar still seemed open. No one wanted to hear that there would be a hefty tab to pay—not the investors, not the regulators, and not the media covering them—so no one said it loud enough to be heard.

What we've seen in both examples is that management allowed a worst-case scenario to persist, paralyzed to change course or address it head on. As we factor in the growing legal expenses paid by all companies in a more litigious society, we find ourselves at the exact moment in our shared history in which communication skills have become, more than ever, a necessity for survival. They've been devalued and underfunded within the corporate structure, resulting in a management class that lacks the tools it needs to address the facts on the ground when called to do so. Corporations lack the full reach of a communications department, integrated within the highest levels of decision making within an organization, to be proactively deployed for outreach, just as executives lack, on an individual level, the communication skills necessary to function at a high level in making the decisions that will substantiate their message.

The result thus far has been flawed messaging that exposes the company to media scrutiny and litigation. When the fear of either outcome results in "no comment," the cycle deepens. Before we look at concepts and strategies for breaking the cycle, we should turn our attention toward what may be the most dramatic example of one company's failure to realize the importance of understanding their audience to strategically communicate during a crisis. What followed was a communications strategy so ineffective and seemingly incompetent in its execution that in every utterance, it only succeeded in channeling the anger and blame of the viewing public back at itself.

3

The BP Disaster in the Gulf and Rampant Groupthink in the C-Suite

Two great disasters in American history caused, at least in part, by groupthink gone awry, were the failure of intelligence at the Bay of Pigs in 1961 and the American military's overconfidence that led to the successful Japanese sneak attack at Pearl Harbor in 1941. In terms of how the facts on the ground were read (or misread), both of these events may have been topped in failure by British Petroleum's (BP) 2010 Macondo well blowout in the Gulf of Mexico. BP stood at the center of its own scandal as millions of gallons of oil poured into the Gulf of Mexico following the explosion of the Deepwater Horizon rig. It was as much a corporate disaster of massive proportions as an environmental one. This was such a huge crisis that from the beginning, no one argued whether present management could survive. The only question filling the financial press was who would and should be the new managers.

There was no way that things could be easily papered over after the explosion and spill. Something had gone very wrong at the executive level, and the way the whole situation was handled approached pathetic and pitiful proportions—leaving a corporate giant humiliated. As top executives kept downplaying the seriousness of the problem in the face of clear evidence to the contrary, it suggested they were living in a closed land of wishful and insulated thinking. Crisis public relations man, Michael Gordon, told Reuters, "BP's handling of the spill from a crisis management perspective will go down in history as one of the great examples of how to make a situation worse by bad communications." Gordon went on to assess the situation, observing:

> It was a combination of a lack of transparency, a lack of straight talking and a lack of sensitivity to the victims. When you're managing an environmental disaster of this magnitude, you not only have to manage the problem but also manage all the stakeholders.

MISSTEPS

CEO Tony Hayward floundered from the beginning. He first called the spill "relatively tiny" and minimized its environmental impact. In light of reality, the statements—at best—lacked credibility and raised extreme suspicions. Oddly enough, Hayworth had come to his post with the promise that the culture of cost cutting at the expense of safety, which had plagued the giant, would be overhauled. Clearly, on the face of it he had failed at this, and then, in its almost amateurish efforts to make the problem go away with happy talk, BP looked laughably out of touch. BP was already fending off a reputation as a serial safety and environmental offender, especially since federal regulators blamed the firm's incessant cost cutting for a 2005 refinery blast that killed 15 workers in Texas and significant pipeline leaks in Alaska in 2006. Hayward's first reaction of blaming Transocean, the firm that operated the rig for BP, and saying it was "not BP's problem," immediately raised flags.

Henry Sneath, who is with an organization of U.S. corporate defense lawyers, explained it to Reuters this way: "In such an awful and public situation, to immediately blame someone else, even if you're right, is bad from a public relations standpoint." He added, "You immediately blacken your reputation and poison potential jurors that might ultimately rule on your faith."

Some of it reflected cultural differences. The United States fancies itself to be a democratic culture, where every man and every woman is an equal. There is democracy in England as well, but it's a democracy that, at least in theory, involves a monarch. Thus, it is much more conservative. It is more hierarchal. Class differences, on all sides, are celebrated in English culture. Workingmen are proudly working men, and aristocrats are proudly aristocratic. It turns out that as unpopular as Hayworth was in America, he was quite popular in England, where he is still treated by the people and the press with a great deal of deference and respect. In a real sense, you can see groupthink at work here on a national level, as the social dynamics of the room (or, in this case, the entire country) dictated a course of action that failed to account for the reality of the situation.

To most Americans who critiqued the government for its lax and indeed, licentious oversight of BP, the fact is that BP had massively lied nearly every time it talked to anyone—including the government. In a document it filed a month before the blowout, it claimed it would be able to remove more than 490,000 barrels of oil a day, should there be a need. That proved to be a ridiculously inflated figure when reality hit. And even after the spill, when scientists asked for BP's help to investigate how oil and gas behaved under water at great depths, their requests were simply ignored. BP operated in the clutches of groupthink at its worst, removing themselves from the conversation without offering any potential solution to a problem they were at the center of, out of fear that their offering would somehow further expose them to liability. Yet, a publicly-held company's fortunes rise and fall, not just on its actual products but also on how people perceive it. Prevarication does not help one's reputation; it makes even a powerful corporation look incompetent. It leaves perception open to a worldwide public audience, which includes not only a general population of at-home media consumers but also those who work in the media, along with CEOs and other senior management, investors, boards of directors, and lawyers. Among these groups is a savvy range of personalities highly capable of determining when they aren't getting the truth, and that lack of transparency will have repercussions.

When Hayworth went yachting, it implied that he lived in a universe where everyone he knows belongs to Boodles—the 17th-century country club in London, originally formed by the landed aristocracy, as a place where they could find the company of their own kind. As the American public watched the spill play out on television, most of them identified with the wives who lost their husbands in the explosion. Many were then appalled when they turned the channel to see Hayward complaining about wanting his "life back"—the takeaway was that from Hayworth's perspective, being hounded by the press while yachting, was comparable to a widow's suffering. When other top BP executives talked about how much they cared about the "little people" as the great spill was still unfolding, it was not merely odious to many Americans; it was offensive.

INDEPENDENT COMMUNICATIONS

While the notion of executives caring for the "little people" and lamenting their missed peaceful yachting opportunities as the great spill was still unfolding proved offensive to Americans, the English understood that aristocrats feel entitled to do such things while the "little people" suffer. Everything here is, of course, relative to whose perceptions we're talking about.

This brings us to the question of communications—usually the Achilles heel of the boardroom. An independent communications department is essential to corporate governance, even if it makes that governance more complicated. You cannot manage corporate communications without knowing the players in the corporation and understanding the roles each has to play. To comprehend the delicate balance that separates successful corporations from their unsuccessful brethren, you have to understand not just the CEO and the board of directors, but also the potential class action plaintiffs.

At BP, it was obvious that the lawyers were ruling the roost, and their recommendation was to repeatedly say, "no comment." From a legal standpoint that might be appropriate; but from the standpoint of a firm's reputation, it's the worst thing to do. "No comment" is interpreted by most people as "guilty" of whatever one is charged with. Surely BP had some competent communications people, but if so, they were obviously relegated to a second-class status and not taken seriously as a part of management. It looked like the nervous lawyers were calling the shots. Admit nothing, they said. So the publicity people wrote press releases that said nothing or said things that were plainly just not true or irrelevant. Instead, the communications people should have had a real strategy for communicating, in both good and bad times, prior to the crisis.

An independent communications center has to be proactive. To build an effective communications strategy, you need an honest and independent assessment of the situation designed with one thing in mind—you want to determine exactly where things stand. You need to do this to provide a sound basis for an effective strategy. The primary thing your strategy needs is a set of actions or statements that are fully mindful of the pitfalls voiced by each vested group within the organization, but aren't beholden to them in communicating a message that's ultimately in the organization's best interest. If we can't say anything out of fear we will be sued, understand that saying nothing costs us our business anyway and does not give us the opportunity to defend ourselves. The only option is to make the best statement possible. Leaving the task of devising such a statement to anyone but a communications expert is a recipe for disaster, as fear and ignorance will make it much more likely that some form of groupthink will take hold. We see it all the time when lawyers take the lead on communications for a company and repeatedly fail in their attempts to communicate their thinking to the larger universe. They may craft a response that from a legal perspective conforms to every item on a list of needs, but an untrusting public inevitably sees right through it. Their failure to communicate should be no surprise—when you aren't trained in these skills, you don't develop them.

When a company honestly audits itself and its overall image, it must look at everything: the good, the bad, and the ugly. Only with all sides accounted for can you develop a strategy that acknowledges the difficult issues you have to work on, as well as the rumors and the lies that should be confronted. As a communicator, your company has to deal with the perception people have of you, even when it is negative. Then you have to work on repairing it, whether it's true or false. If it's true, you have to repair the problem itself; but either way, you have to shift the perception.

Not being strongly aware of the role communications must play in a modern corporation's survival strategy can lead to excessive groupthink, as—without either strong communicators voicing logical arguments internally, or professionals in place to lay the groundwork for media management before things escalate—the path chosen is usually the one of least resistance, conforming to the best case scenario or overcompensating to avoid the worst. None of this is easy to achieve. When the rubber hits the road, executives have to decide how much independence their top communications man or woman should have.

Look at the important role of independent communications in corporations. To manage corporate communications, you have to understand the players inside the corporation and their roles in creating a solid reputation. You have to look closely at the CEOs, CFOs, senior management, corporate lawyers, boards of directors, corporate communications and investor relations officers, and externally, at the company's audiences—the media, class action plaintiffs, and Wall Street money firms that influence, through the media, how the company is perceived in the marketplace. BP is, of course, an example of a spectacular corporate failure, on many levels. But failures also occur in other examples on a lesser scale. Unfortunately for them, the stiff upper lips the BP executives maintained proved most attractive internally, even though the approach utterly and completely failed to inspire confidence externally. The takeaway isn't that a stiff upper lip approach is always fatal—after all, had BP been addressing an exclusively British audience, the tactic may have been exactly what the situation called for. What you need to learn from BP is how essential it is not only to know who is going to respond to your message before you give it but also to identify potential audiences prior to the worst case scenario happening so you can formulate a plan under unstressed circumstances. As it played out, BP should serve as an example of what not to do in a communications crisis.

Months after it happened, commentator James Carville appeared on CNN and talked about the BP spill, saying that the level of distrust against the company had grown even more intense. The outrage was escalating as the public saw the millions of dollars the company was spending on its own television image, instead of on helping the people and economy, which had been devastated. You can bet that companies in deep trouble that get called out for attempting to rehabilitate their image too soon have not maintained independent communications departments with any real power; if they did, the first order of business would be to help rectify the situation itself, so that efforts spent on image could be backed by facts. Usually, such departments are relegated to a second-class status. The ideal thing, of course, is for the communications department to be a real part of management. Undoubtedly, a firm like BP has good people in its communications department, but it's a good guess that they weren't allowed to do their jobs.

Communications departments should be brought onto the level of senior management for the sake of strategizing, and not just to crank out press releases. Inherent in this communications process is educating senior executives on the difference between publicity and public relations. Publicity is primarily a one-sided endeavor to get a message out to audiences. Public relations involves crafting messages to target audiences as part of a larger dialogue. The former puts forth a single statement and when done skillfully, can lead to greater exposure and understanding of what the company is about. The latter is a larger process, which for each step, must ensure that its messages are: understood by the sender (the corporation); received and understood by the receivers (different audiences); evaluated; and ultimately result in a response message or feedback from the receivers. Once the communications process can complete this cycle, a symbiotic, open relationship between the corporation and its audiences has been created. To keep the cycle from being disrupted, senior management must fully understand what is trying to be achieved in communication campaigns initiated during times of distress, calm, or opportunity. Failure to understand what's at stake at any given point in the process will prevent buy-in and allow groupthink to derail the effort.

Once your communications department has a seat at the table, you can seek out their input on a real strategy for communicating to your audiences in good and bad times. Ideally, you need a senior vice president of corporate communications to meet with the heads of industrial and investor relations, to gather perspectives from both camps, when contemplating the most appropriate strategy. You need perspectives from investors, employees, and the consumers of your products to understand where the true pain points are and how they need to be addressed. All these people need to put their heads together when crafting the appropriate communications for your company to function properly.

EQUAL FOOTING

An effective communications strategy requires independence and an evolving, honest assessment of where your company stands from multiple perspectives. From these things, you will then have the basis for developing your underlying theory on how to proceed. It is important that after doing its due diligence, your communications department has the ability to craft a message that truthfully speaks to its audience in the most effective way.

Every interest represented at the executive meeting table could, and probably will, have some resistance toward the elevation of a communications leader (as I have already alluded to, there is an across-the-board deficiency in communications skills). There should be no wonder why such a professional might stand at the opposite end of skeptical peers. The BP fiasco illustrated that one of the greatest challenges to effective corporate communications usually comes from legal advisors. In order for an organization to engage in meaningful communication with a targeted audience receptive to its perspective, it cannot have its message distorted by lawyers at every step of the way.

You have to keep your legal team in check, even if their training has generally not equipped them to deal with communications on an equal footing with their own set of skills. It's a paradox of their profession, which they must learn to deal with and executives in the boardroom must uphold. Why legal, specifically? Because part of their role is that of protector, and from their perspective, the less said on sensitive topics, the less that can be used against the company. Internally, what may be a matter of practicality for a lawyer may be received as a message driven by fear. When members of the management team, unskilled in communications, accept the notion that "saying the wrong thing will lead to bad things," then saying nothing at all begins to look like the best option. Just as no one wanted to tell the Wall Street crowd that the party was over when it came to credit default swaps, no one wants to support a strategy that could lead to the worst-case legal scenario. The difference is that where an unskilled communicator might be overwhelmed by the notion of "saying the wrong thing," a qualified communications professional at the executive level has been trained to know the difference and must be seen as an authority, to provide balance against a potentially over-defensive legal perspective. As much as this book has advocated the elevation of the communications executive, balance must be achieved for the group dynamic to be effective after reorganization. Knowledgeable professionals from multiple disciplines must contribute to the discussion so a well-informed decision can be made. If the equilibrium is disturbed and one voice becomes so dominant that it is the only viewpoint considered, it might, once again, allow for groupthink to infect the process.

$$* \quad * \quad *$$

When large corporations, such as Toyota and BP, are accused of wrongdoing or sued in a court of law, there is always an assumption of guilt; the role of the senior communications executives is to take the lead in making certain that the corporation's messages are heard, read, and understood. As we now begin to turn the corner in our discussion and start to focus on what makes communication effective and what companies need to do to embrace it, we will look at those companies that succeeded where Toyota and BP failed.

4

Effective Corporate Communication at Work

The corporate communication failures that served as case studies for the opening chapters of this book were chosen because they provided an easy frame of reference for a larger discussion. These meltdowns unfolded on such a large scale that you'd be pressed not to have had an opinion of each while they were developing, and the common threads they share begin to reveal a pattern where smart, talented executives repeatedly fell into the same decision-making traps.

In each instance, we've made reference to different forms of groupthink that either stifled communication or created the conditions by which the worst possible decisions seemed appropriate. When communication strategies don't seem like strategies at all, or when they fly in the face of logic, we now have some idea as to where to look to identify the cause of such missteps: a lack of education as it relates to communication skills and a management structure that does not include an independent communications group. The objective for the rest of this book will be to illustrate the process by which the two primary contributing factors to ineffective communication and the groupthink that makes it possible, can be corrected. Just as the previous case studies provided examples that allowed us to identify what's wrong, this chapter will look at companies and leaders that used corporate communications effectively as our model for the solution.

FEDEX: THE RIGHT MESSAGE ON TIME

The difficulty in selecting corporate role models for their handling of a crisis is that, by design, they're harder to remember. We remember the catastrophes for a reason—mostly because a potentially emotional story with sensational elements inhabited our media space for an extended period—but, if a communications strategy has helped a company successfully navigate around a crisis, we're supposed to forget it.

During the 2011 holiday season, the purchaser of a new computer monitor had his package delivered via FedEx. When the carrier encountered a gated fence surrounding the customer's house, rather than ringing the bell he threw the box over the top and walked away. Not only was the intended recipient home at the time "with the front door wide open," he also caught the entire incident on a surveillance camera and posted the video to YouTube (FedEx Guy Throwing My Computer Monitor: http://www.youtube.com/watch?v=PKUDTPbDhnA).

Within 48 hours, it had gone viral, making the leap from being watched by YouTube viewers to being shared on social media. Already, over 2.4 million users had seen the video, and—if the typical progression happened here—next, mainstream media would be broadcasting it on both morning and evening news. Three days after the video posted, this is exactly what happened, doubling the total views online to over 4 million—on top of those who had now seen the footage on their televisions.

Before things escalated to a national level, FedEx took action. Within the first twenty-four hours, they had already begun their response: first, through traditional media, a spokesperson was quoted in the *Daily Mail* expressing shock at the incident and vowing that "this won't be [the carrier's] best day." As the video itself was beginning to get traction on social media, the response included an active Twitter presence: FedEx made it clear in a series of tweets that they had seen the video and would be addressing the situation. By day two, they had successfully connected with the customer, apologized for what had happened, and made arrangements for the monitor their driver had damaged to be replaced. Then they went back to Twitter to get the word out that they had in fact made good on their obligation.

Right away, they had a positive outcome to attach to the existing story, which would be one of the key takeaways from any retelling. Finally, they built on all of this with a direct response. Senior VP Matthew Thornton III recorded a video of his own, also posted to YouTube, entitled "Absolutely, Positively Unacceptable" (FedEx Response to Customer Video: http://www .youtube.com/watch?v=4ESU_PcqI38). In it, Thornton again delivered the message that the customer at the center of this had been met with face-to-face, apologized to, had received a new monitor, and was fully satisfied with the outcome. Thornton also shared his own disappointment and embarrassment over what transpired in the video, distanced those actions from the majority of his team, and reassured his customers that he had made certain that the video has been shared across the company to remind its employees how important every package was.

Thornton's video was posted just as the original video was making the first rounds on Facebook, but before it hit the

Today Show and other morning news programs. His team recognized how bad it would be if any broadcast airing of the damaging clip suggested that FedEx couldn't be reached for contact and erased that possibility from the narrative. Now, if the viral video of a FedEx employee behaving badly would become a national news story, it would do so with the ending they wanted people to hear already written.

More than that, every element of FedEx's response shows how well they knew their audience, and that they were able to use their message to address everything that audience needed to hear. The target audience was, first, their customers, many of whom could be imagined to have watched the video wondering whether their holiday purchases would meet a similar end. They also had the potential to relate to the recipient of damaged goods so well that they could be angry for him. FedEx gave them a messenger in Thornton who in a moment of transparency, took responsibility and admitted embarrassment over what he saw—making himself entirely relatable in the process. He erased the specter of the faceless corporation ruining Christmas by emphasizing that the situation had been resolved personably and satisfactorily. Why would anyone be angry for the original customer, if it were now clear that he was happy with the outcome? Why worry about your own gifts in transit, if FedEx is clearly the kind of company that takes care of their customers?

Beyond those customers, the quarter of a million FedEx employees worldwide, trying to do their jobs during the busiest time of the year, were also paying attention, and they heard their professionalism defended. Investors following along, wondering whether this could develop into a scandal with long-term implications, heard that management was taking the bad actions of one employee and turning them into a learning experience the entire company could benefit from. This is how you craft and target a message, backed with immediate action, that allows the messenger to take control of a potentially damaging story before it gets out of hand. FedEx was never going to stop the video from spreading, but they defused the circus sideshow that might have accompanied it. In the process, they may have even tapped into a new audience, with over a half million people actively choosing to seek out and view Thornton's response—a one minute and forty-three second commercial touting FedEx's values and standards.

FAST FOOD, FAST RESPONSE

Separate incidents, involving two fast food chains, each pick up on one of the primary traits that allowed FedEx to escape its potential crisis relatively unscathed—speed. One of the telltale signs of groupthink is paralysis in the face of a crisis. It is the same type of paralysis that prevented Kennedy's advisors from voicing dissent prior to the Bay of Pigs, and which produced a muted response from Toyota as their hard-fought-for reputation was being demolished on a daily basis. The likelihood of creating a response that is both effective and decisive becomes severely diminished when the management team responsible for acting is overwhelmed by fear or a lack of communication-driven leadership.

Papa John's

Papa John's is a national franchise of take-out and delivery pizzerias that bills itself as providing "Better Ingredients, Better Pizza." Unfortunately, if there were a better customer experience attached to that promise, it escaped the cashier at a

Manhattan location, whose take-out receipt for one customer included a racial slur as a customer description. The outraged customer posted a picture to Twitter, along with the message, "Hey @PapaJohns just FYI my name isn't "lady chinky eyes." The well-known conservative politics of Papa John's CEO John Schnatter made them a ripe target for many to promote the tweeted image as a correlation between such politics and insensitive behavior, and the image went viral on both Twitter and Facebook. A timely response was paramount, as anything less would have fueled a narrative that Papa John's was indifferent to racism.

The original tweet was posted on Friday night, and—fortunately for Papa John's—their communications team was already in place and robust enough to deal with it right away. By Saturday, Papa John's had reached out to the slighted customer over Twitter, apologizing and asking her to give them a way to contact her directly. As angry observers responded to the original tweet, the Papa John's team was able to step in, inform them that they were on top of it, and make it clear that the cashier was being fired.

Papa John's was able to act quickly to avert a disaster. More significantly, their team was already in place and engaged with social media. This wasn't a corporation scrambling to figure out whether and how to respond; Papa John's public relations team was prepared to act, and did so over the weekend—as opposed to letting it fester until Monday morning when it might have been beyond their control. Structurally, the authority was either there or granted to them not only for coordinating an effective response but also for dismissing the offending employee. What's clear is that as a company, Papa John's buys in to the value of effective communication, giving their staff the opportunity to succeed.

Taco Bell

There is an implicit trust which must exist between diners and restaurateurs for hungry patrons to choose to eat out instead of cooking at home. That which is on the menu must be an accurate representation of what is served. Scandals over substandard meat or unsavory substitutions have been known to inspire a "better safe than sorry" response for many would-be consumers, who will stay away at the first whiff of impropriety. This was the potential crisis Taco Bell's management team faced upon the filing of a class-action lawsuit against them that claimed the fast food franchise was engaging in false advertising by referring to their taco filling as "seasoned beef," and that the fourth meal snack of many a late-night patron "does not meet the minimum requirements . . . to be labeled as 'beef.'"

Ouch!

The lawsuit wanted Taco Bell to "stop saying they are selling beef," creating an instant punch line for anyone looking to take a cheap shot at cheap food. Claims like these, if left unchecked, can forever brand a product in the eyes of some consumers. Today, look no further than Ikea meatballs, and those who will forever associate the once-guilty pleasure of many a suburban furniture shopper with the horsemeat they were accused of cooking with, to appreciate the potential damage Taco Bell could have suffered. This lawsuit spoke to the core of Taco Bell's identity; it was the culinary equivalent of suggesting that Toyota produced unsafe cars. Unlike Toyota, Taco Bell's answer would be both swift and loud, matching the severity of the accusation with the boldness of their response.

The original stories about the lawsuit included a first-round response from a Taco Bell spokesperson, denying the claim and promising a vigorous defense. Within twenty-four hours, Taco

Bell followed up with a statement from their President and Chief Concept Officer, Greg Creed, promising to take "legal action for the false statements being made about our food." The message was clear and simply stated: Taco Bell's accusers had "got their 'facts' absolutely wrong." There's no wiggle room in Creed's statement, no games of semantics, and—at face value—no lawyer-speak red flags for the media and the public to jump on.

Of course, while official responses from company presidents carry authority and can reach a sizable audience and reassure many of their concerns, they don't generate headlines in the way accusations of fake meat do—and for much of the public, those headline accusations were potentially the beginning and end of the story. To reach that audience, the would-be customers who were turned off by the question that the coverage—at a glance—forced them to consider, Taco Bell would need a headline of its own.

Four days after the news of the lawsuit broke, Taco Bell took out full-page advertisements in the *Wall Street Journal*, *USA Today*, and *New York Times*, among others. The headline, in big, bold type read: "Thank you for suing us." The ad continued, delivering "the truth about our seasoned beef," with a series of statements and facts describing their process and standing behind their product. Taco Bell's original statement said the lawsuit against them was false; their follow up built on that with a cheeky headline that became news unto itself. Considering the younger demographic of a majority of Taco Bell's customers, the tone of the ad's title spoke directly to them, and the content of its message effectively rewrote the story. In response to the accusation that they used less than 35% beef in their mixture, Taco Bell went all in with the statement that the real mixture was 88%, with the rest of the filling consisting of seasonings, spices, and water. The narrative now had a beginning, middle, and end, as the suit was dropped a few months later.

The lawsuit against Taco Bell had no specific damages attached to it, which made it appear to have been a gambit for a settlement that would put an end to the bad publicity. The counteroffensive not only incorporated strategic use of communications but also required an assessment of whether the company president would be able to function as the face of the defense, authoring both an early statement that set the tone for the argument ahead and the larger advertisement that would turn the corner on the story. The only way Taco Bell could have put itself in the position it did, within a week of the announcement of a potentially damaging lawsuit, was if its communications team not only worked with legal but also took the lead in crafting an authoritative response.

MGA vs. MATTEL: THE MEGA TOY WAR

This mega toy war trial started in 2008 and lasted several years. Tom Nolan, a top litigator for the global law firm of Skadden Arps, Slate, Meagher & Flom, represented MGA Entertainment in its battle with Mattel over the rights to Bratz dolls in federal court in Riverside, CA, an outlying city and county bordering Los Angeles County. Nolan brought me into the case to craft a litigation public relations strategy in the belief that a proactive strategy with the media would be crucial to fighting Mattel. Mattel had been extremely aggressive in the case, and Nolan knew he had to do something. "It was imperative that our side become proactive in telling our side of the story to the global media since the court of public opinion was important in reaching out to all of MGA's target audiences," Nolan said.

Nolan was amazing to watch. Over the years, he had developed excellent relations with the financial and legal media and a reputation as a top litigator. He had a stellar career of super trials with corporate defendants as clients. He and his colleagues were, and still are, considered the "go-to" law firm when litigation hits a corporation, and their client base includes many Fortune 500 companies listed on Wall Street, as well as numerous private companies.

One of Nolan's greatest accomplishments during the trial was the way he used the resources at hand to begin to change the conversation in the media. Nolan invited Nicholas Casey from the *Wall Street Journal* to the Skadden offices, where MGA CEO Isaac Larian wanted to present his case for the court of public opinion. I was assigned to prep Larian on the importance of staying on message. The resulting front-page story in the *Journal* went global, and that one story successfully shifted the tone of the public debate. It was a blockbuster article that transformed the debate, from a copyright issue, to one in which Goliath—Mattel—was portrayed as trying to burn down David's—MGA's—home. Suddenly, everyone everywhere had gotten the message MGA wanted them to get. We worked on clarifying it in meetings between Nolan, myself, and Larian, but the article and the narrative it created set the stage for the two-month trial that followed.

Until that point, Mattel had been assertive in portraying the trial in the court of public opinion as one about intellectual property rights. Nolan understood the importance of managing communications for MGA. Ultimately, MGA Entertainment came up with attention-grabbing headlines, with a federal filing that rewrote the story: "Everything Mattel did was to deceive a federal judge into believing Mattel was good and MGA was evil," the filing alleged. It accused Mattel of vigorously promoting itself as an ethical company when in fact, this was not the case.

MGA accused Mattel of having spied on rival toy companies for more than fifteen years in an effort to defraud other companies of secret details about more than fifty products, including the famed Bratz line. MGA showed that Mattel executives had gotten workers to print up fake business cards in efforts to infiltrate rivals' private showrooms as a "market intelligence" group, which sent employees on regular trips to toy fairs across the globe. They were looking for everything—from product ideas to advertising strategies—using fake credentials to get in, and signing nondisclosure agreements they had no intention of honoring. Instead, they relayed their findings in reports to the C-Suites, which were ultimately reviewed by Mattel CEO Bob Eckert.

During the deliberations, I convinced David Colker, a *Los Angeles Times* reporter covering the trial, to write a piece focusing on Isaac Larian's incredible life story. Colker detailed Larian's coming to this country from Iran as a refugee, working at a restaurant washing dishes while he earned his college degree, then building MGA Entertainment into a successful toy company. The resulting headline was "The All-American Toy Story." Getting an effective human interest story out on my client and against Mattel, with the powerful global Weber Shandwick public relations firm representing them on the other side, was a key component of turning and winning the public relations battle for MGA during the first trial.

While the lower court ruled that MGA had to pay $100 million in fees and the judge eventually added that the Bratz dolls were to be given to Mattel, the 9th District Court of Appeals in California unanimously overturned the verdict, 3-0, in my client's favor. And, in a second trial that followed in 2011—I did not participate, but they followed my media training—MGA Entertainment not only won big in a unanimous decision, but the court also ordered Mattel to pay MGA Entertainment $309 million dollars, including legal fees. The 9th Circuit reversed $172 million in damages (for trade secrets claims), but upheld Judge Carter's award of $137 million in attorney fees, and that number has survived. It was a resounding victory for MGA Entertainment and was greatly trumpeted in the financial media, both nationally and globally.

Correct messages are crucial when a corporation is embroiled in litigation. Messages must use the right words, pictures, and actions to convey their true meaning. Messages are so crucial for a corporation in a distressed situation because it is the only way to get to the court of public opinion. But—don't forget—of all the factors determining how persuasive corporate messages are, how it's perceived is the ultimate goal, and the credibility of the source is key. When you put an executive in front of the media, you unleash a high-risk/high-reward situation. Is your CEO credible and trustworthy? The more believable an executive is, the more he or she will be able to get the message accepted.

It's amazing how some of the biggest and most powerful corporations become so mired down in groupthink and a shelter mentality in a crisis. Their messages are so badly crafted that essentially nothing is communicated. And that's never good. When you're trying to persuade people of something, you have to have something to say. Denial or no comment is dangerous stuff to shovel at the media. Reporters are often proud of their ability to detect BS, and there's nothing that elicits a negative response quicker than the smell of something that registers unusually high on the old BS meter.

Although the nature of media is itself undergoing a transformation, it remains the gatekeeper of the messages corporations depend on for communicating with their internal and external audiences. It's no news to any CEO that a reporter, editor, or producer will not always write or report exactly what you need to get out in your message. A good corporate executive should be trained to understand the ebb and flow of interviews, and a savvy CEO needs the backing of a well-versed financial public relations professional. The CEO will need to hear a real professional's views on how to craft the message, along with the key strategies and tactics needed to get that message out successfully. If financial communications executives are doing their jobs correctly, they will maintain excellent media contacts with the appropriate trade and financial media. They also need to know the major newspaper, magazine, broadcast, and cable television reporters intimately. They need to know how to get benchmark coverage.

I saw first-hand how Nolan deployed both legal and communications-driven attacks in his strategy for serving his client. To me, he represents a cross-disciplined evolution that is necessary for the modern professional to thrive. In his appreciation for the importance of a strong communication presence while operating as a legal authority, he was able to use tools from both areas interchangeably, bringing me in so that his press outreach might influence the trial, while later using a legal filing to further drive home the message he wanted communicated.

STEVE JOBS

Any look at corporate communication done right, along with any mention of a possible evolution in leadership, will come to its natural conclusion at the highest representation of communication leaders of the modern generation—Steve Jobs. Contrary to the typical path to leadership, with its emphasis on accounting and financial skills, Jobs brought a keen appreciation and understanding for marketing and communications to his post. He maintained an open-door policy for communicating with the media early on, and it paid off. After John Scully fired Jobs from the company he founded in 1985 (years later, Scully would suggest it was only a demotion), Jobs' relationship with the press, and his savvy in how to approach it, kept most of the negativity out of the coverage. He refrained from being connected to any criticism of Scully, and was generally treated well in the write-ups that followed. Over the next decade, he pursued several worthwhile projects before coming back to Apple and forever changing the device landscape.

AntennaGate

Jobs was broadly praised for his ability to communicate his vision to a mass audience regarding the Apple products developed during his tenure. He turned announcements that would have been treated with wonkish-level coverage into media events. Macworld and the World Wide Developer's Conference still attract thousands in attendance every year, along with simulcast coverage on Apple TV and websites, and live blogging from every corner of the web—all to tune in to a corporate presentation.

The media, the financial press, and the customers all believed in Jobs's Apple, and while their successes have been well covered, perhaps the greatest testament to Jobs's ability to command the conversation can be gleamed from Apple's failures. In 2010, the release of the iPhone 4 came with the usual fanfare—which is to say, excessive excitement accompanied the company's first major redesign of its flagship mobile product. The product debut was the centerpiece of a typically hyped Jobs presentation, as "the best iPhone ever"—with its slightly more industrial design, faster speeds, more impressive display, and better battery life, it was poised to take the mobile device market by storm. Only, there was one small problem.

Upon first contact with the next generation smartphone, the tech blog community began to remark on what it perceived to be a problem. The remodeled phone had moved the antenna, so that it ran around the device's edge, and users began to identify a holding position from which the signal would be significantly dampened. Signal bars were dropping with the wrong grip, and "AntennaGate" was born. The facts would suggest this was a nonissue, as some blogs demonstrated that a user's hold affecting a smartphone's signal was pretty common, and—despite the controversy—the launch was successful, with over 1.7 million iPhone 4s sold in its first three days on the market—making it the most successful iPhone to date. But the questions persisted, and whether it was the backlash of the greater spotlight reserved for Apple products, or the simple appeal of a "mighty have fallen" story, "AntennaGate" had legs.

What's most interesting about Apple's response is that they were right on time in getting a message out in their own defense, but many observers scowled at its content. Unhappy users received an e-mail from Steve Jobs suggesting they hold the phone differently, and other Apple statements suggested it was a software problem. Over the next three weeks, Apple took some hits, with competitors seizing on the scandal—including Motorola, who included a copy line in a full-page *New York Times* ad for the Droid X boasting that its antenna was "the kind that allows you to hold the phone any way you like . . ." *Consumer Reports* reviewed the device and cited the antenna as cause for not recommending it, and when the software update did arrive in the form of iOS 4.0.1, it succeeded in preventing the bars on the display from dropping, but did nothing to improve the signal when the "death grip" was applied.

Finally, Steve Jobs stepped forward and called a press conference to address the issue. Jobs understood that there was a problem, but he also saw that the story was a more significant problem than his phones. There was no *mea culpa*, no recall; instead, he simply set the record straight. He confirmed that the issue with the iPhone 4 was a demonstrated problem across the device category and provided data to illustrate how infrequently the problem occurred, the relatively low level of actual complaints, and the decreased number of returns with the current iPhone in comparison with its predecessor. Finally, he left his audience with the message that "We're not perfect. Phones are not perfect. We all know that. But we want to make our users happy." Anyone that was actually unhappy over the performance of the iPhone 4 could request a free bumper case that would alleviate the issue.

The critics suggested that he broke all the rules, that he should have apologized, that he came off smug, and even that he was the ultimate media manipulator, but in my opinion, there is a part of our culture that sometimes demands a pound of flesh when it can get one. Jobs recognized this, and although his situation was comparable to Toyota's—insofar as the allegations against his product may have been blown out of proportion—he realized that his reputation would let him set the record straight if he leveraged it properly. A transparent announcement on a large stage, which didn't risk an insincere apology to distract from the facts, proved to be the way to go. For proof, all we need to do is look back and see that "AntennaGate" was proclaimed CNN's "biggest tech fail of 2010," and yet within a year of Jobs's statement, Apple's stock price hit over $369 per share. Based upon its market capitalization at the time, the company was the most valuable corporation in the United States, having surpassed Exxon Mobile.

Knowing Your Audience

Apple's dominance under Jobs was a testament to not only having brilliant intellectual capital and products but also, as demonstrated, having an understanding of the important role of open communications. Steve Jobs was the master of effective corporate communications, he knew how to wield it, and he knew his audience. Now not all corporations will necessarily be able to hire unusually effective communicators to head up their enterprises, and even Jobs did not always succeed, but he made sure he was communicating openly. His leadership was perceived as a driver of the company's success, having brought the company back from near-bankruptcy, and it was no surprise that when the first story of his health issues began to surface (with his surgical leave of absence), the market reacted negatively, and in the immediate wake of his 2011 death, Apple's stock dropped 5%.

Steve Jobs and his bearing on Apple's share price highlight for us, the audience to corporate communication that sits apart from the public at large, the importance of both the message and its effect. Every public company must balance the egos in the boardroom against the opinions of legal council and the potential reaction from the world at large, and it must do so knowing that investors are watching. Often, the message to the public is targeted at the investor but gets lost in the static of ineffective communication or drowned out by the volume of unintended response.

In the wake of the worldwide financial meltdown and a rapidly changing environment, where social and commercial media collide like thunderclouds, we need a new investor relations and public relations paradigm. The whole attitude of corporate communications needs a shift the likes of which most executives will resist—but they will do so at their own peril. There is little sense in treating institutional investors as important and serious, with a cogent and significant investor relations program, but having little or no financial public relations (PR) campaign in a crisis. The convergence of PR and investor relations (IR) has become so important that failing to combine the two functions can drive a public company's share price down. Steve Jobs understood this, and his response to AntennaGate was as much an effective means to defuse a runaway story, as it was a message to investors that there was nothing wrong with Apple's products. Jobs knew that he didn't need to apologize and give birth to a new headline, which would potentially trigger market uncertainty. Instead, he presented the facts transparently, without giving up his position. He reminded everyone watching that the bottom line had not suffered, despite the volume attached to the outcry, and he was ultimately proven right as both the customers and Apple's investors believed him.

Today it is a fiduciary responsibility of senior management and the board of directors to ensure that PR and IR have seats at the decision-making table, while making sure their opinions are valued and heard. Corporate boardrooms need to establish new ground rules for effective communications, and to do that, corporate America must develop a new breed that is talented in the necessary disciplines.

In Part II, I will review the theories that define our understanding of modern communications, and outline and argue for the claim that battling groupthink requires a greater understanding of communications as a discipline and the convergence of public relations and investor relations. Combining these two functions will help eliminate groupthink when you need to get out key messages to your target audiences, both internally and externally. The PR-IR Nexus strategy, understood in the context of the Shannon-Weaver model of communications (detailed in the next chapter), will be our roadmap toward remaking corporate America. Throughout the remainder of this book, I intend to demonstrate the effectiveness of this approach.

Part II

Theories and Paradigms

5

The Role of Communication Theories

Why do venerable corporations, such as Toyota and BP, fail miserably when it comes to communicating in distressed situations? There are legions of public relations professionals working within the corporate structure and a multitude of outside public relations firms, all of which provide advice to the executives of these companies. But, year after year, mistakes are made in the communications process, which cost the boardroom millions to correct. The problem lies within the corporate communications paradigm in boardrooms across the country and around the world and to a minor degree, the crisis communications industry itself.

There are many qualified public relations professionals nationally who are sought out to provide crisis advice and initiate campaigns to help resolve the negative issues involved, and a sizable shelf of books on both the successes and failures. Among them, you'll find more than one on the Exxon-Valdez disaster, in which millions of gallons of oil spilled into pristine waters off the coast of Alaska. You would think that with twenty-four years of hindsight at their disposal, BP would have learned a lesson on how not to communicate in a crisis from the Exxon spill. The confounding issue is that corporations, small and large, deal with problems and potential crises every day, from disgruntled customers and unhappy investors, to shareholders who demand better returns, and employees who harass other employees—the list is endless. But when it comes to an external crisis such as a recall, spill, or unsavory stock trades, these Ivy League MBAs become immobile and repeat the same mistakes in communicating to the public: groupthink and silence.

The Institute for Crisis Management lists four potential causes for a corporate crisis:

1. Human error: an executive or an employee commits a major error, which causes an unfolding crisis to escalate.
2. Technological or mechanical problems: an airline, for example, does not use correct maintenance, which causes an accident, or an employee hijacks a computer for sensitive information to sell to a competitor.
3. Acts of God: hurricanes, earthquakes, floods, and the like disrupt operations.
4. Boardroom decisions: senior-level executives don't take the problem seriously enough or defer it to some other executive.

The problem with all of these crises is that they attract public scrutiny from a fourth estate: the media, whose primary responsibility is to serve as watchdogs for society and its citizens. As the news coverage grows, it can have the debilitating effect of disrupting business as usual and can generate political, legal, and financial actions against the business. The problem with crisis communications plans is that they leave out the cause and only focus on the effect, which is why groupthink is so prevalent in corporate boardrooms.

From the case studies reviewed in Part I, we drew two conclusions from the successes and failures we observed. One of these is that for many corporations, the structures in which they operate prevent solid communication advice from ever surfacing in their actions. With the volumes of information on the Exxon-Valdez disaster for BP's team to draw from, the right information could not break through the internal threshold, from which ideas are promoted to policy. Instead, BP's decisions were weighted down by the influence of internal groups, which did not grasp what they were allowing to happen by potentially marginalizing communication efforts.

The ease with which communications can be discarded is a result of our second conclusion—namely, that the influencers within management have not been properly educated on the complexities of communication as a discipline. To many, it is a soft concept relegated to support staff rather than a driving force for change. We saw in the last chapter just how powerful effective communications can be during a crisis or litigation, and how great corporate leaders can reap significant benefits when effective communication is a component of their arsenal.

It is my belief that for today's companies to be prepared for the world around them, they need to have among their leadership ranks, those who possess critical communication skills and those that have been educated in the science of communication. The former is a subject tackled later in this book, but the latter needs to be detailed here, as it forms the basis of the arguments and proposed solutions to come.

COMMUNICATIONS 101

Let us now get down to the basics. The first step to rooting out groupthink among brilliant executives in the boardroom is to look at the underlying theories that have formed the communications paradigm, as they evolved from the art of rhetoric to the models that propelled our greatest technological advances of the twentieth century's latter half. There are several communication theories that help us better understand the act of communicating and the target audiences we are trying to reach with our messages during a crisis. Reviewing them here will give us both a foundation for the discussion to come as well as an appreciation of what professional communicators bring to the table.

Aristotle

Aristotle's *Rhetoric*, more than 2,300 years ago, laid the foundation for modern public speaking and communication. He stated that the most important part of communications in the public arena should include three rhetorical proofs:

Ethos (ethical)—the speaker must be ethical
Pathos (emotional)—the speaker must persuade an audience
Logos (logical)—the speaker's actual words must follow a logical progression.

Without all three rhetorical devices working in concert, the speaker's messages will not be received or understood by their audiences. Aristotle was the first to understand that the duty of a rhetorician was in identifying with an audience: their perception of the speaker or the one communicating messages matters.

Norbert Weiner

As an academic field, communications, which was mostly known by the odd term "information technology," grew out of the mind-numbing work of Norbert Weiner, an MIT mathematician. In part, Weiner was educated by Bertrand Russell, the great English philosopher and mathematician. One of Weiner's profound truths is that "information is information, not matter or energy." He was really the first person to see what computer technology would do in the coming decades. He developed a field called cybernetics, which is about machines making machines, raising questions about the role of humans. He developed an avid interest in communication theory, out of which cybernetics grew. His early interest in all this centered in how communication works, for man and for machines. He was an early advocate of robotics and automation, believing it would enormously improve people's lives.

Weiner was an enormous influence on many scientists in his time. It is said that his work had a profound impact on Claude Elwood Shannon, the mathematician who developed information technology. Wiener's work in mathematical probabilities and entropy were said to influence the Shannon-Weaver model of communications, which talks about the source of information, how it is transmitted and signaled, how it is received, and the message itself.

SHANNON-WEAVER

In 1948, Claude Elwood Shannon, a mathematician, wrote *The Mathematical Theory of Communication* with Warren Weaver, who helped make it accessible to the non-mathematician. It was first published in the *Bell System Technical Journal* and then as a separate book. In his discussion of information entropy, he used Wiener's mathematical work in probability theory—although there is much debate concerning how much influence Wiener really had on the Shannon-Weaver paradigm. For most of the 1950s, the connection was assumed. Shannon, like many of post-World War II America's greatest scientists, was a research scientist for the Bell Telephone Company. He developed a mathematical theory of signal transmission originally designed for telephone lines. Shannon wanted to achieve maximum telephone line capacity with minimal noise distortion. He never intended for his mathematical theory of signal transmission to be used for anything but telephones. In essence, when Warren Weaver applied Shannon's concept of information loss to interpersonal communication, one of the most durable models of communications was born.

The Shannon-Weaver model assumes that a message needs an information source and a sender. That message is relayed through a channel to a receiver. The message is usually encoded

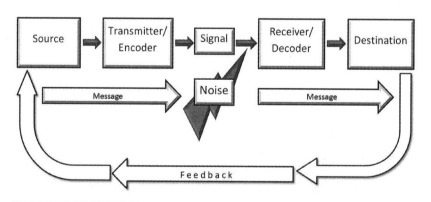

A depiction of the Shannon-Weaver communication model, as it is understood today, illustrating the delivery of a message from source to destination with the inclusion of a potential feedback route from which the source may appraise the response to its efforts.

for its journey to the receiver, but it must pass through noises of various types, produced by various interferences. Then when the message is received, the receiver has to let the sender know the message was received as it was intended, which means: the message must be decoded and the receiver must provide adequate feedback.

That is, in essence, the formula. Each part of this model is crucial, and incorrect use of any component can result in total communications failure. And you can see that a mathematical theory, created to deal with something as prosaic as a telephone line, laid the foundation for effective corporate communication for decades.

Both in its original form and in modern variations, communications theory sees the sender as having the primary responsibility for the success or failure of the process. But in a corporate environment, something else develops—something that Shannon-Weaver calls "noise." Noisy lawsuits, noisy employee demands, noisy corporate crises—all can hinder the communication's path. As a result, a corporation's customers and vendors may begin to question whether the corporation will survive.

Shannon-Weaver postulates that the encoding is important because it is the process during which the source takes an idea or thought and selects how to create a message that is accurately transmitted to its intended audience. Encoding is important so that culture, gender, education, language, and life experience in general are correctly included. The next step after encoding is a crucial one. The CEO has to understand how the message should be understood by its audience. During litigation, restructuring, or any crisis, senior executives must be clear about what they are saying—if they hope to rally public opinion to their side.

Thibault and Kelly

The early 1950s was a fertile time for the development of the concepts of communications theory. In 1952, John Thibault and Harold Kelly, both psychologists with strong interests in sociology—in particular, group dynamics—wrote a seminal book, entitled *Social Psychology of Groups*. They elaborated on a social exchange theory, which said you could use the economic model of costs and benefits to predict human behavior. The next year, Kelly wrote *Communication and Persuasion* with Irving Janis as a coauthor. In later volumes, Kelly also tackled the psychology and sociology of attraction, love and conflict, in an effort to catalog personal relationships. He retired as one of the celebrated psychology professors at UCLA, outliving Thibault. Their work evolved into a social exchange theory that assumed that individuals and groups choose strategies based upon what they see as costs and rewards. This is an important theory, which influences communications, because the social exchange theory postulates that people and groups factor in consequences of their behaviors before acting.

The Social Exchange

My own take on this is to argue that in communicating a message, both the sender and the receiver want to weigh the benefits and costs of the communication. And when a corporation gets mired in groupthink, the message usually gets encoded incorrectly. Encoding is typically where groupthink sets in and makes it difficult to either craft the correct message or send out anything that will ensure a corporation's reputation stays positive.

A perfect example of this is that of Richard Fuld, former CEO of the now-defunct Lehman Brothers. Fuld and his senior management presided over the largest bankruptcy in American history, a $63 billion debacle that shook Wall Street to its core. Fuld failed to understand the importance of encoding when communicating to internal and external forces. Throughout 2008, rumors had been spreading on Wall Street that Lehman Brothers was highly leveraged and in debt, especially in some of its Orange County operations. Known on Wall Street as the "gorilla," a kind of testimony to the nature of his reputation, Fuld hid himself from the media and his own employees and insisted, from afar, that these were only rumors. He then seemingly just plain lied about how well the firm was doing.

Fuld made it all worse by remaining invisible. Compounding the issue was his allegedly abrasive management style, as too many other executives and politicians, who felt he had crossed them, were rooting for his downfall. For Fuld, the chickens were coming home to roost. When things started to deteriorate even further in the summer of 2008, he resorted to stirring up a groupthink environment of "us versus them." Fuld did such an incredibly poor job in communicating to his own employees that when the end was at hand, they learned about it with little warning. Fuld's denial of the seriousness of what Lehman was facing, and the willingness of those around him to buy-in to such a flawed—when weighed against the facts—message, was both a groupthink response in decision making as well as a demonstration of how such a poorly encoded message becomes impossible to clarify until the bottom falls out: If we all believe in the lie, maybe the lie will somehow prove to be true, and everything will be okay; if we dig at the inconsistencies and seek out the truth, we'll have to accept how dire our situation really is.

David Berlo

In 1960, David Berlo expanded on the Shannon-Weaver linear model of communication and created the sender-message-channel-receiver model of communication. Subsequent scholars added the important issue of nonverbal communications—which comprises the majority of communication between humans and includes gestures, expressions, eye contact, clothing, hairstyle, tone of voice, and range of emotions, to name a few. These theories have set the foundation for practical solutions to helping solve communication breakdowns.

Everett Rogers

Professor Everett Rogers, at the Annenberg School of Communications at the University of Southern California, developed the understanding of how people process and accept information even further. He developed the "Diffusion Theory" of communications, which postulates that people go through five discrete steps in processing information. These include: awareness, interest, trial, evaluation, and adoption. Without being too much the "pop psychologist" here, it is noteworthy that Rogers grew up on a farm, and his father so favored the advances made in farming tool technology as a result of increasingly sophisticated mechanical and electrical devices, he was blinded to developments made elsewhere. Unfortunately for Rogers's father, the most significant advances in the 1930s in Iowa were in biology and chemistry—new hybrid corn seeds. So, while the neighbors on adjacent farms were getting 25 percent larger yields with more drought resistant crops, Rogers's father was not ready for the drought of 1936 and went bust because he badly misread the times.

Rogers decided to study how people get ideas, and then how they communicate them. Upon his return from the Korean War, he studied sociology and statistics. Later, he tried to figure out—as best he could—how business executives make the decisions they make. Diffusion theory looks closely at the components of corporate communications and for that reason, is important to study.

The first place your audiences will probably hear from you is in the mass media. Executives have to state their cases in the court of public opinion in such a way that they get people's attention, from opinion makers to the average Joe on the street. You want to rally opinion makers to your side right off the bat. The court of public opinion is reached through mass media. If people are convinced, you've done fine. If they hardly notice you, that is not good; and if your message isn't convincing enough to rally public opinion, you have communications problems. You have to arouse your audiences—internal and external—otherwise, your corporation is vulnerable, especially in times of crisis. To survive in the public marketplace, your audience must empathize with your position.

Kenneth Burke

Kenneth Burke was a literary and rhetorical theorist who contributed to the evolution of rhetoric and communications, over a life that spanned a full century. His foundation in this area stemmed from his belief that human action is essentially symbolic action, shaped and motivated as if it were a drama; hence, he became known for his "Dramatism Theory." He emphasized that all of life and communication is a drama, and his primary concern was with the communicators' ability to identify with an audience. His dramatism theory identified five elements:

1. Act—the communication
2. Scene—the context background for the act
3. Agent—the communicator performing the act
4. Agency—the means used to achieve the act
5. Purpose—the stated or implied goal of the communication.

In communicating, he believed that human action is essentially symbolic action, shaped and motivated as if it were a drama—which a crisis of any kind is. In his classic work, *A Rhetoric of Motives*, Burke wrote that rhetoric or persuasion is essential to the study of the human condition. Rhetoric preserves or alters social order by influencing the way people perceive their symbolic relations.

Walter Fisher

Walter Fisher is a key figure to the history of communications because he believed that all communications are forms of storytelling—a kind of "Narrative Paradigm"—where people are essentially storytellers, and messages are best understood as stories. Two aspects compose the test of this model:

1. A communicator must examine narrative coherence because this determines whether the story holds together and whether it makes sense in our world.
2. A communicator must check the narrative fidelity. Does the communication match our own beliefs and experience? Does it portray the world in which we live?

His narrative foundation of communication is based upon the notion that people are storytellers and tend to make decisions on the basis of good reason. Fisher believed that history, biography, culture, and character determines what counts as good reason and that the world is a set of stories from which we choose—and this, on a consistent basis, recreates our lives.

Marshal McLuhan

Marshal McLuhan, the Canadian media philosopher, wrote in his seminal 1964 *Understanding Media* "in a culture like ours, long accustomed to splitting and dividing all things as a means of control, it is sometimes a shock to be reminded that in operational and practical fact, the medium is the message." This is truer today than it was then, given the Internet, social media, twitter, blogs, and the lightning speed with which messages are now sent globally. The medium has become more crucial than ever: when someone needs to send a message, and someone else has to receive a message, the medium determines how the sender gets feedback. You want the receiver to be able to interpret the message correctly—as the sender intended in the way it was encoded. The right channel is paramount to the success of a communication from a corporation. It's a process with many variables that can interfere with the outcome: consider the complications people's past experiences, education, language, gender, culture, and social system introduce.

APPLIED THEORY

In a crisis, the executive must understand that communication is an activity in which important information is conveyed. Actually, the word communications is derived from the Latin word, "*communis*," which means to share. It is also imperative to understand the rational world paradigm when communicating: namely, rational people make decisions on the basis of argument, and the type of situation—such as a crisis—determines the course of argument. The upshot is that the world is a set of logical puzzles we can solve through rational analysis.

In litigation, restructuring, and other crises, a corporation's ability to send its message correctly encoded and ready to translate is essential. Of course, the message a corporation sends will often not survive all the variables. The message may not be understood. That of course, is why feedback is necessary. Without feedback, you don't know whether your communication was successful.

Once the sequence for how communication is constructed is understood, a new set of keys for proper application arises. If our examples earlier in the book successfully answered the question of "why" effective communication is necessary, and the theories profiled here represent "how" communication functions, then our next step is to look back on those theories and concentrate on "who" communicates. Who is the best source for communication within a corporation? What they say and when they say it will be determined by an honest appraisal of the situation at hand, and the specific identity of "who" will be the face or voice of a particular message will be determined by the actual situation, but as an authority and a source of information, it is essential that—in both crafting and delivering a message—the source be able to best represent narrowly targeted interests. These are the same interests that Matthew Thornton of FedEx and Steve Jobs of Apple tapped into in their messaging—namely, those of the investors as well as the public. In the next chapter, we will discuss the importance of the public relations-investor relations Nexus as a model for independent communication units and as an essential tool in achieving buy-in for both individual messages as well as for restructuring the corporate boardroom.

6

The Evolution of Public Relations into the PR-IR Nexus

The rise of public relations as a profession correlated with the rise of mass circulation newspapers and magazines, from 1900 through 1917. During this period, known as the "Seedbed Era" in American corporate history, there were fifty well-known magazines with circulations of more than 100,000—remember, there was no television or Internet. *Ladies Home Journal*, which was founded in 1883, had a circulation of close to 1 million. The muckraking journalists of this era—Lincoln Steffens, Upton Sinclair, and Ida Tarbell, among others—used these national public forums to rail against the abuses of big business and corporations. This was also a time when high school education had become compulsory in America, and literacy rose dramatically, which helped build a growing middle class that wanted to read about consumer purchases and luxury items. Along with millions of immigrants (mostly Europeans) coming to America and learning about citizenship, English, and commerce through the public schools and the media, there was definitely a communications revolution going on; companies, corporations, and the government were eager to use public relations as a way to send their messages out to an eager public.

THE RISE OF PUBLIC RELATIONS

Corporations at this time, in general, had policies of not commenting to the press, and of course, there was no Securities and Exchange Commission to require accurate disclosure. But as negative stories started coming out from the muckraking journalists, the public attitude toward large enterprises darkened, and their reputations started to decline with the buying public. President Theodore Roosevelt still figures prominently in history for his legislation against "robber barons"—corporate entities—and for his trust-busting endeavors against the oil companies, steel corporations, and railroads. One could argue that he understood the value of public relations and made his campaign public to pressure these conglomerates. Corporate America learned a lesson—no one is above the court of public opinion in this new age of the national media. A number of public relations specialists arose who became seasoned at working with the media on behalf of corporations.

Ivy Lee

One of the first serious practitioners of proactive public relations on behalf of corporations and companies was Ivy Lee, a former journalist. He helped pioneer the field of public relations by attempting to represent corporations in an honest and professional manner. In the early 1900s, Lee issued a "Declaration of Principles," which set the professional standards of modern public relations, and he mailed his manifesto to all relevant editors of newspapers and magazines. These principles are so good that they should be read by every corporate public relations executive in America today, 100 years later. In part, it read:

> This is not a secret bureau. All of our work is done in the open. We aim to supply news. This is not an advertising agency. In brief, our plan is, frankly and openly, on behalf of business concerns and public institutions, to supply to the press and the public of the United States prompt and accurate information concerning subjects, which are of value and interest to the public to know.

Lee was among the first public relations professionals to issue "press reports," which we would classify as news releases today, to reporters on a large scale. Among his clients was oil tycoon John D. Rockefeller, Jr.—who, at the turn of the 20th century, was a favorite target of Ida Tarbell, the skilled investigative reporter and muckraker. Tarbell wrote the *History of Standard Oil Company*, in which she lambasted both Rockefeller and Standard Oil. Lee was successful in helping to "balance" Rockefeller's image in the national media, by skillfully representing Rockefeller's business accomplishments and philanthropy to journalists.

Edward Bernays

The father of modern public relations was a man named Edward Bernays. Interestingly, the double nephew of Sigmund Freud, Bernays developed an understanding that the unconscious could be influenced with messages to sway public opinion. Bernays started practicing public relations in the early 1900s and continued providing public relations counsel to corporations, individuals, and governments until his death in 1995, at the age of 103. In many regards, Bernays laid the theoretical groundwork for the field of public relations in 1923 with his seminal work, *Crystallizing Public Opinion*. This work remains the "bible" of public relations. With this book and others, Bernays went on to teach the first academic class on public relations at a New York University in the 1920s. Much of his work remains cogent today, insofar as it recommends proactive public relations when representing a corporation. Heavily influenced by his famous uncle, Bernays understood that people could be persuaded—if the messages sent to them supported their beliefs, values, and interests.

Bernays pioneered the technique of using "third-party authorities" to plead his clients' causes in the court of public opinion. "If you can influence the leaders, either with or without their conscious cooperation, you automatically influence the group in how they sway," Bernays wrote. He understood early on that good public relations professionals could become "influencers" for causes and public opinion, especially in crises. His clients included President Calvin Coolidge, Proctor & Gamble, Dodge Motors, and other American and foreign corporations. To this day, when corporations commission "independent" studies to help in fighting crises, they are following in the footsteps of Bernays.

Arthur Page

Another pioneer in the field was Arthur Page, who became vice president of public relations at AT&T in 1927. Over the next two decades, he was set apart with his insistence that his department act as interpreter, from the public to the company and vice versa; he set up the first two-way communication system for gauging public opinion.

PUBLIC RELATIONS TODAY

As important as these pioneers were, it is equally important to remember that they operated in an era before the huge upsurge of the financial media: the *Wall Street Journal*; global financial news wires, such as ThomsonReuters; Dow Jones; and particularly the electronic media, including search engines like Google, and independent blogs.

The public relations profession is changing rapidly and gaining respect in the boardrooms of both corporate America and the rest of the world. Bernays and Lee would be impressed by how the reputation of the field is being elevated, especially in the legal arena of the federal courts. In a groundbreaking ruling in a New York federal court, a judge ruled that legal advice, which is intended to shape public opinion and is part of the discussions between lawyers and public relations executives and individuals under investigation, is now protected under attorney-client privilege. The ruling is significant to corporate boardroom executives because, with what seems like weekly scandals brewing in corporate America and on Wall Street, public relations executives with an expertise in crisis and litigation have become crucial to managing corporate risk, as it relates to reputation, and are fast becoming sought after.

Another component to this evolving landscape is that the financial and business media outlets market their anchors or journalists like rock stars with an incessant demand to fill the "news hole" with content. On a more substantive level, financial and business reporting has never been more sophisticated or trenchant, certainly at premier publications, such as *Forbes*, the *Wall Street Journal*, *Bloomberg/BusinessWeek*, *Investor's Business Daily*, the *New York Times*, *Financial Times*, and the *Economist,* to name a few.

Corporations must now operate in a global market where the mass media—including the social media—can spread bad news about executives, companies, and their products and services in the blink of an eye. In the half century since Marshall McLuhan popularized and defined the terms "mass media," "global village," and "Age of Information," one could argue that his assertion, "the medium is the message," has never been truer. With the global expansion of business and financial news on cable outlets and the Internet, the medium plays a leading role in shaping public opinion about scandals wracking public companies globally, while analysts and journalists monitor how these corporations respond or act during a crisis or litigation. Once these articles are written and archived, they can be found on the Internet and are accessible to reporters, investors, and the public—worldwide.

Consider the flood of financial television shows—such as those on CNBC, Bloomberg News, and Fox Business News, combined with the important role that news wire services, such as Dow Jones, ThomsonReuters, and the Associated Press—play in disseminating good and bad news about companies and their respective scandals to a global audience. This has been especially significant since September 15, 2008, when Lehman Brothers collapsed and caused a tsunami of bad news, which rocked financial markets from the United States to Europe and Asia. This mass medium can be as slickly staged as a Broadway production and provides viewers—investors, other boardroom CEOs, and the global financial media—oceans of bad news on the financial information of public companies and their management, as well as on the surrounding regulatory and business environment.

The communications failure of companies—such as at Toyota and BP—was not only a misfire of corporate communications during a critical period but also a failure to understand the importance of having a communications strategy that works to deal with the *causes*, not just the effects, of corporate communications problems. This has been the problem with most crisis reactions from the corporate boardroom. There are numerous crisis communications specialists, who ply their trade by writing and implementing crisis communications plans for corporations—costing hundreds of thousands of dollars—but the problem with most crisis corporation communications campaigns is that they don't go to the root of the problem, which is getting the corporate boardroom to unshackle its groupthink mentality when a crisis hits.

There is a new public relations and investor relations paradigm that effectively deals with the causes and effects of crises in corporations, the issue of groupthink, and helps public and private companies navigate the minefields of corporate inaction: the public relations-investor relations (PR-IR) Nexus. Rather than making hype the goal when combating a negative perception in the marketplace, the new way of doing things is to tell the truth and be as transparent as possible. We have already seen effective applications of this principle in Chapter 4, specifically in the cases of FedEx and Apple.

Taking the effective possibilities already illustrated to a scalable solution (after all, not every company will have a "Steve Jobs" at the lead to effortlessly amalgamate the needs of different audiences into one message), I recommend that in distressed situations, the thousands of public companies listed on Wall Street consider coordinating, if not proactively merging, their public relations and investor relations functions. There is little sense in treating institutional investors as important and serious through a cogent and significant investor relations program, while having a Wild West crisis public relations campaign underway.

When public relations and investor relations are coordinated, it provides a powerful incentive for board members to listen with credibility to what will happen if there is no independent, coordinated message coming out of the corporation. Public relations and investor relations executives must gather the intelligence that will allow them to provide the correct information on the situation, conduct a thorough analysis of it, and execute a proper response; it must become a cause that makes senior management take notice and accept the disastrous nature of inaction or "no comment."

How is this achieved? If the financial books were in question, a careful review of the ledger would go a long way toward bringing to light any misallocation of resources. Corporate communications should be no different. An internal and external communications audit, which can be done *quickly* and *efficiently*, will provide the boardroom with credible evidence to act appropriately. In the equivalent of a 9-to-5 work week, with about 10 hours of initial investigation and 30 in follow-up, the case can be built to convince any company that responding in a proactive manner with a media strategy based upon rigorous intelligence gathering will make a difference—with the financial media, in neutralizing groupthink, and in helping to handle the unfolding crisis. We will detail the steps of a communication audit in Chapter 8; for now, the takeaway is: to deliver a transparent message, an honest assessment of the situation must be made first.

CONSTRUCTING A NEW PARADIGM

The meeting of public and investor relations into a PR-IR Nexus will create a new paradigm to help shape the analysis that will lead to a successful resolution of potential crises and the elimination of groupthink from the corporate decision-making process. Viewing crisis management through the lens of public and investor response will, first, hasten the understanding of the problem within a company by focusing the team on finding the key drivers creating it. Then, the big picture can be viewed with those drivers in mind to foster the development of rigid, fact-based solution proposals. Each formulated solution is a hypothesis to be tested, and doing so will ultimately lead to results that invite the entire process to repeat on a more focused level, slowly breaking groupthink's hold on the communications structure in the corporate boardroom in the process.

Every crisis encountered, including those similar to the case studies in this book, will require the same style of analysis on a situational level. Taking a step back: in order for a company to be as self-reflective as it needs to be to come to the honest conclusions this process demands, we have to apply the same methodology to the corporate structure as a whole. Here, we already know the thesis, as the preceding chapters have identified the drivers of poor communications decisions in multiple examples. It bears repeating that the common thread to the case studies in Chapters 1–3 is: highly intelligent executives, who run corporate boardrooms and generate large profits for shareholders and stakeholders, measurably fail when a communications or litigation crisis arises.

This basic theme has resurfaced throughout our argument, and facing it is the first step to understanding how prepared your company is, should it be exposed to scrutiny. What it says about your business is: it doesn't matter how smart your people are, how fine their pedigrees are, or what you think of them personally; how well they respond as a group, when the world is watching, depends upon both their understanding of communication theory and their willingness to see whose strengths make the greatest assets in each particular set of circumstances. Embracing this line of thinking will provide senior management with a road map to ask the hard questions and perform the fundamental analyses to get to the correct solutions. It will also help in avoiding the "red herrings" that pop up to divert an executive from the core issues—this approach will help keep management from the wrong path and stay focused on the problem. Because this is an initial hypothesis, it will help frame the problem and lead to fruitful research and discussions that lead to a solution.

As companies and the leaders within confront this likely truth, it will force them to dig deeper—what are the drivers leading to failure among their executives? Is it a deficiency in talent development, a failure of diversity in promotion when it comes to skill sets, rooms full of "yes" men and women with polished resumes but no incentive to speak their convictions? When the conclusion can be drawn that one of these scenarios is present within a company's key decision makers, or any combination of them, we must dig deeper again. What decisions, policies, or patterns got us here? What have we been overvaluing to create our current circumstances? Later in the book, we'll look at some hypothetical scenarios and walk through an analysis of each one.

THE MARKET VALUE OF A NEW PARADIGM

The convergence of the resources in public relations and investor relations has become so important that not combining these functions could have negative consequences for a public company's share price when a distressed situation hits. In today's turbulent marketplace, it is the fiduciary responsibility of the boardroom and senior management to ensure that what this new paradigm communicates to a company's varied audiences during a crisis is, in fact, solid. As seen by the communications of those company failures we've profiled, powerful PR machines can easily collapse under the combined weight of a relentless media pursuing a story, alongside regulatory agencies and elected officials pressured to investigate. In each of the companies we've looked at—and countless others that continue to make front-page news—mixed messages were sent to the investor communities and to the national and global media.

The market capitalization of companies is increasingly determined by "intangibles." Good intangibles can be solid senior management, a board of directors that is credible in helping guide the corporation in growth and profitability, employee satisfaction, and ethical-but-profitable business partnership arrangements. In particular, the market needs to know whether the management and the CEO can be trusted. Are the accounting procedures and investments factual and true? Some market studies indicate that as much as 40 percent of a market's capitalization is determined by these intangibles—this percentage is probably even higher in the post-financial collapse era we live in today. So, when investors or buyers of a company's products or services are looking to do business, a typical company's book value represents about half of the company's capitalization. Trust and value generate and maintain goodwill toward a company's messages, products, or services in a distressed situation.

That is what intangibles get a company, especially in a crisis or a litigation which can ruin a company's reputation. When a company is sued or an investigation is commenced, in today's climate, there is an implied perception of guilt in the court of public opinion. What helps is the intangibles the company has built up over its business life cycle, assuming these are positive like the ones listed above. Earlier, when we mentioned the necessity of a communications audit, we stressed the fact-finding portion as being key. As we'll discuss later on, an audit can be conducted before or during a crisis, but the substantial benefit in doing the work beforehand is that it is the best way to actively manage your way toward the goodwill you will need to survive when the bottom seems to fall out. In other words, if you know where you stand, you'll know where you need to improve before it's too late.

The stock market perception of intangibles could account for half of the share value of a publicly traded company, meaning how a corporation responds to a crisis, and specifically media inquiries is vital. Like it or not, we are now in a 24-hour global news cycle: the financial media plays a crucial role in determining perception, and management is often perceived as either innocent or guilty through the lens of the financial news media. Just as embarrassing viral videos and tweets can penetrate the mainstream media and prompt action, the financial media can pick up on stories of mismanagement, restructuring, or larger developments and dominate multiple news cycles with coverage of them. The resulting obligation of senior management and the board of directors is to make sure that the investor relations and public relations teams are, in fact, on the *same* team, especially during a crisis or litigation. As a result, I would argue that we are entering into a "Golden Era of Public Relations," where crisis management, not publicity, must be the focus of communications and reputation rebuilding for corporations.

Crooked corporate management, bogus accounting practices, the selling of faulty mortgages that received the top grade from ratings agencies, and the recurrent Wall Street obsession with quarterly earnings statements have made for an equities and bond market that is as volatile as any in memory. Consequently, managing public relations and investor relations without groupthink is especially necessary in these choppy waters.

Although it may be self-serving to say so, the awkward situation that corporations find themselves in plays to the benefit of the public relations and investor relations professionals, who now have key roles to fill in educating investors, employees, the financial media, and yes, the most important audience for buy-in—the board of directors. These professionals will have to intelligently argue that strategic positioning and long-term development of the company's fundamental messaging will be the value drivers for the present and future. Further, they must make the case that only by taking stock in itself and realistically evaluating how the company is perceived, will its executives be able to use that awareness to shore up and enhance the company's reputation as part of a regular and active campaign. It is this actively managed reputation, along with strong support from the board of directors, that will allow them to successfully navigate a crisis or litigation. It will always behoove a company to be above board and transparent, as it helps in gaining trust from the "groupthinkers" in the corporation who are frozen by indecision; but, with a flood of new regulations coming out of Washington, such behavior may in fact, one day be mandatory.

GATEKEEPERS OF REPUTATIONAL CRISES

It was only a few years ago that corporations viewed public relations professionals as nothing more than those who sent out news releases—more tactical than strategic. Similarly, investor relations officers were seen as disclosers of company numbers and handlers of the "dog and pony shows" on Wall Street—but not anymore. Given the volatile nature of crises, the distrustful public, and elected officials who are compelled to acquiesce to up-in-arms constituents—lest they face their own reputational crisis—public relations and investor relations professionals are now the gatekeepers in handling the agenda and flow of crisis and litigation.

This team must also decide—with board approval—the corporation's story lines in a crisis or litigation. Shading stories for audiences or the financial media does not hack it anymore. In addition, and just as important, the team must actively put senior management before the media for interviews, making sure everyone is clear on both what to say and what not to say when the company is in litigation. Naturally, it will help if senior management members are charismatic, but intelligence and earnestness will carry as much weight on most days.

The public relations and investor relations team must also convince the board of directors that running a public company inevitably entails public obligations, especially during a crisis or litigation; it is much like holding public office. Ultimately, anything that hurts market capitalization—and it can go into a downward tailspin in a crisis—is a breach of fiduciary responsibilities to shareholders, employees, and external audiences. At times, getting the board of directors to get out of groupthink can be difficult because most of the members are accustomed to being answered to, not the other way around. In a crisis, it must be communicated that the corporation is unwavering in its devotion to transparency and has a board of directors that is independent and forthright. This golden age of public relations has been a long time coming as the public relations executive moved from the newsroom to the boardroom. Now in the role of a gatekeeper, he or she must use the skills and knowledge of communications to manage the flow of information coming out of a corporation while handling external requests for media coverage.

* * *

At this point in our discussion, all the pieces we need to move forward should be in place. We've identified the problem facing modern corporations by looking at those who have failed in the public sphere, and used the success of others to illustrate how effective the proper use of communication can be during a crisis. At the center of this discussion is the repeated observation that groupthink can insinuate itself among talented professionals and impede progress by preventing them from making well-reasoned decisions. We've argued that, through education and restructuring where communications professionals are placed within an organization, we can nullify the presence of groupthink from future critical decision-making moments. To the former, we sought to reach a greater understanding of the communications process and used it, in concert with an advocacy for the convergence of public and investor relations, to begin the groundwork for the type of messages we want our companies to deliver.

The goal is: transparent and targeted communication crafted by an independent communications team represented within management. Finding a way to get there, with full organizational buy-in, is the objective of the chapters to come. In Part III, we will take the lessons from our earlier studies and apply them to a hypothetical company, allowing us a real insider's view on where things go wrong, and a framework from which we can argue how to remake corporate America so that it might survive the changes in media and public perception that define our modern age.

Part III

Remaking Corporate America

7

Anatomy of a Crisis

We've seen over and over that the smartest people in the room can still get it wrong when it comes to dealing with a crisis under a media microscope. The problem is, no one thinks it can happen to his or her company. Maybe we look at these crises as they unfold and assume bad luck or a media vendetta, or maybe we just know we're better than the poor sap whose spokesperson is getting lampooned on every outlet while the company's stock takes a dive. Maybe we're right, but risking an organization's reputation or its very existence on a "maybe" is a good way to find yourself in the next roundup of bad examples for others to learn from.

So, if it's always the other guys, then where do they go wrong? The examples we've explored in the previous chapters all highlight near-fatal decisions that soured the public on their respective makers, but for an alternate path to make a difference, that path needs to be an option in the first place. That one bad move can stain a reputation and lead to all of the ramifications discussed, but it's not enough to say that the companies we've looked at chose "A" instead of "B," so don't choose "A," and you'll weather the storm just fine. When major decisions must be made, the choice that represents the values championed in this book must not only be proposed but also must result in buy-in. In other words, if you put this book down believing that elevating a single communications expert to an executive level will save your company, then you've missed the point. To change the room that makes the main decisions, you must first go into your organization and change the culture that created it.

Perhaps you read that last sentence and scoffed. "There's nothing wrong with our corporate culture;" or "We hire the best, that's what got us here;" or "A corporation's culture is a reflection of its leaders, and as one of those leaders I'm proud of what we've made and what we stand for." This may all be true, but the call to change the culture isn't a moral judgment; it's a business decision. Toyota's culture was celebrated for how it valued challenge, teamwork, and respect, among other characteristics—all noble qualities, none of which helped them in 2010, as their reputation was smeared across the media and around the globe (although it can certainly be argued that Toyota's way allowed them to make the changes they've made since their ordeal to pave the way for their recovery).

The need to change the culture within is driven from changes to the culture around us. Bloggers on the Internet need something to blog about, 24-hour news stations need a story to cover, scandals drive hits and ratings, and references to the same can be broadcast at a rate of 5,000 tweets per second. Nowhere in challenge, teamwork, respect, and the remaining stated Toyota values of improvement (*kaizen*) and empathy (*genchi genbutsu*) is there an ingredient that can stand up to the tide when it's bearing down.

Once you accept that seemingly smart, well-run companies with noble values can still be blind to modern vulnerabilities, you might permit yourself a closer look at your own organization. Of course, the question that naturally follows is "What are you looking for?" I believe the best way to recognize the areas of deficiency, which can leave even the most celebrated companies exposed, is to create an example. In the remaining pages of this chapter, we will look at a fictitious company and explore how the values that built it may be traditionally positive yet fail to meet modern needs. Ultimately, we will see that these same values will produce a culture that is not only bound to repeatedly make bad decisions in the spotlight but will also fail to recognize when the full gaze of the spotlight is about to be pointed in its direction.

HIRING

There is no more direct representation of your values than the people you choose to bring into your organization. With every vacancy, the resumes that cross your desk are an opportunity to introduce a new perspective and expertise into your workplace. Polished candidates with proper pedigrees line up at your door and wait for you to decide your definition of "the best." And if you've made your decision according to the same logic that has been in place for generations, you've given weight to prospects who attended the most prestigious schools and worked for the most impressive organizations. You've narrowed down your pool, through references and colleague recommendations, and your final decision probably came down to which applicant gave the most memorable performance during the interview.

When the process is complete, and you've had your offer accepted, you can sit back and congratulate yourself for having done the necessary due diligence required to get the best people working beneath you. Not only that, but you've helped create and maintain the hiring model for the rest of your organization. And the truth is, there's nothing wrong with the process. Many great workers and leaders have both been found and found their place through the same ritual. You can get to the end of this book, buy into every idea put forth in it, and still end up hiring the same types of candidate for certain positions, more often than not.

That said, in this scenario, because you didn't emphasize communication skills to your hiring manager, you shouldn't be surprised that once you see your shiny new employee in action, she performs exactly as you'd expect. She boasted of being a whiz with a spreadsheet during your interview, and she is. She's already proven herself to be extremely competent in her daily business, highly efficient, and overall a productive employee. Unfortunately, she isn't as proficient when it comes to staying on message. You didn't notice this during the interview because, in a one-on-one setting, she seemed clear and concise in her carefully rehearsed interview points. When it comes to making a presentation, she seems to hold her own, but when management chooses to steer the corporate ship in any given direction, she never seems to fully get her people on board. At best, she picks up key words from corporate memos and presentations and re-gurgitates them in her own reports, but ultimately, you get the impression that she views your message (or worse, those from your superiors) as a fad or a slogan, rather than an initiative. Your best candidate was never taught to value or respect corporate communication as anything more than a business school elective. She sees it as an obstacle, something in the way of her doing real work—work that she does quite well but with no regard for the evolving bigger picture.

STRUCTURE

The hiring decisions across an organization will influence the corporate culture on a micro-level, but the centerpiece of internal and external communications will be the communications personnel themselves and where they fit into the larger corporate structure. Even the bad company we've created here wasn't oblivious to communications being a piece of the puzzle. They've gone out and made every effort to hire the best people, with every candidate's background once again vetted and filtered, here only those with the strongest of communication skills considered. Historically, they've hired some good people too, competent and well liked. With all appropriate teams in place, how effective they can be is now a matter of hierarchy and influence.

Every department has its organizational chart, a tree of managers and direct lines of reporting, which feeds all the way up the ladder. Vertically, it's easy to see who's in charge, who's subordinate, and where everyone else stands. Horizontally, it can get trickier. Perhaps separate fiefdoms coexist with minimal interaction, save for assigned support groups. Our scenario here will be even more informal, with a half-dozen vice presidents (VPs) reporting to one group president, among them a head of communications charged with public relations for each group. From there, each president—along with Legal, HR, the CFO, and the COO—reports to the CEO. When there is a major crisis or shift in the organization, this management team will be advising on and executing the course of action.

On a daily basis, information and directives get sent up and down our chain of command; just as often, support and service is carried out diagonally within each group. The contracts department makes haste when acquisitions needs them to; perhaps marketing is serviced by a print production group for assets to distribute; and when the head of sales says "jump," most groups respond. Everyone on the ground knows which groups carry the weight, and which leaders have their president's ear; furthermore, their knowledge is confirmed by way of perks, promotions, and access.

In the middle of this is a talented vice president of communications, serviced by a capable team. They've been responsible for branding global marketing campaign initiatives and crafting messages that are vetted from the top down. Of course, the most capable team members are occasionally frustrated by the lack of buy-in among their colleagues. These are the same colleagues we spoke of earlier, whose hiring gave little weight to hard communication skills and as a result, have little understanding of or appreciation for the group's efforts. To make matters worse, turnover has become something of a problem; with top management within the group already in place, rumor has it that the department is something of a dead end, and good people are leaving. That pool of "the best" talent is only "the best talent available," with the newest wave of innovators opting to look elsewhere. The new blood that is brought in to the fold, most familiar and best connected with the latest in social media (having grown up with it), their influence is still minimal, and they're frustrated that their managers—along with those they see to be in power—don't understand what they do.

Now, there's a crisis.

CRISIS

We're most familiar with the scenarios that could be thrown at our company; we've discussed enough of them already to know how they look from the outside. Many in the media, and more at home, ask how corporate powerhouses and industry leaders could let things get so out of control. What was management thinking? How could they not see that they were only making things worse?

The answer, as we've laid it out here, shows that it wasn't necessarily bad or incompetent people leading things astray.

If it were that easy, then it could never happen to you because you'd see them coming from a mile away in your own organization. It wasn't necessarily a lack of talented communications leaders failing to give the right advice or propose the right strategy either; in fact, our fictitious organization has gone above and beyond, with its own VP dedicated to the role. Scariest of all, no matter what skills you value in your staff, how your organization is structured, or what its culture is all about, sometimes disaster strikes—unprovoked. No PR executive or chief communications officer could have prevented the Blackwater explosion. The initial reports on Toyota's problems would have been news regardless of how their organizational chart was laid out.

For our organization, perhaps it was something as simple as an ill-advised comment, tweeted by an employee who doesn't even work out of the main office. Maybe it was racy or insensitive; it could just be a poor attempt at humor taken out of context—but the Internet has noticed, and it isn't happy. Overnight, our company is trending, and the actual source of the controversy couldn't be picked out of a lineup by management. Our legal and HR heads advise that it's an internal matter and should be treated as such. No statement is made, but it's agreed that the offending party will be firmly reprimanded.

The problem is that the initial outrage inspired a handful of resourceful bloggers to dig a little deeper. They've devoted their time to searching old Facebook posts and forum comments, and they found something worse in the process. Now, it's not only a trend; it's a story. Our little company that wanted the best people is suddenly rebranded as racist, misogynist, irresponsible, greedy, or insensitive. Management realizes it won't go away and asks our Communications VP to see that a statement is written. After a handful of revisions and a legal read, our statement is issued, but it's release is immediately accompanied by

101

accusations from an ex-employee of similar insensitivities. The former employee has supplied an out-of-context, but nonetheless damning, e-mail, short enough to be incorporated into hundreds of stories and posts, each tweeted and retweeted thousands of times, extending what has become a national conversation on a story that just won't go away.

While all this is going on—with reports, rumors, and memes flying at the speed of data—business as usual still needs to happen. An underlooked thing that occurs to a company in trouble is the effect on the workforce. Employees are traditionally both the most forgotten audience of a company and the backbone that gives it strength to get through bad times. If a CEO is well grounded in communication skills, this will probably be the first place that will benefit. The employees will have better information, which will aid them in acting and performing in a crisis situation. A huge plus in a crisis is the decision-making abilities of a firm's employees—in little things and in big. So if the CEO is an effective communicator, there will be an immediate effect on the people who make the whole thing work.

AFTERMATH

We can keep spinning our incident further and further out of control, and we can raise or lower the stakes of the initial spark that brought it upon us, but by now the reoccurring beats of a meltdown like this are familiar enough for us to see it for what it is. The crises that befell each of our case study organizations from previous chapters, and affecting our own imagined company here, are forces of nature that strike indiscriminately. Sometimes we see them coming; sometimes we're blindsided; but how we respond is what turns a one-cycle story into how your company is referenced for years to come, and our ability to respond effectively is the result of what we choose to value when things are calm.

The failures in this scenario may have begun when a reasonable social media policy, crafted by a high-ranking communications manager, was ignored. Whether or not the initial act could have been prevented when the storm hit, communications was the arm of the company responsible for crafting a response after the management team bunkered down and agreed that no response was necessary. Each vested group had what they felt was a valid reason for its own group's interests to say nothing.

Even if our Communications VP was brought into the conversation early on, the tenor of the meeting or e-mail chain would have made it abundantly clear that the most acceptable option was to "play it safe." Suggested responses may have been tossed around, but nothing would have been fought for (and if it were, it would have been a losing battle). The person meant to champion effective communication as a strategic response was still the last person invited to participate in the conversation—and the lowest standing member at that. When that voice did join the discussion, it was seen only as the representative of a group defined by the support provided to others, instead of as an authority on a valued subject.

More than anything, this chapter has been built to that last sentence, to illustrate that in otherwise perfectly functional corporate cultures, it will be impossible to have an effective authority on communications help lead the way out of a crisis. The subject isn't valued as it should be because it wasn't factored into the decision to hire or promote either the decision makers or the groups they work with that influence their attitudes. The authority was never put in place ahead of time, so why would anyone recognize it under duress? With no one to lead the way, the team resorts to looking for social cues as a means to consensus—cues dictated by a more narrow perspective or flat out self-interest. Speaking out or strongly advocating alternatives fails to be constructive. The result is groupthink, and the remainder of this book will explore how to identify the areas of your organization most susceptible to it, provide examples of companies whose values and structure have allowed them to avoid it, and the creation of an alternate to this chapter's example, illustrating what our ideal workplace looks like and how it functions.

If after you've turned the last page, your final takeaway is that communication is an essential discipline within a modern organization, then not only will you look to have the roles and influence of your communications-specific personnel be amplified, but your definition of "the best" for every hiring decision will also factor in (or at least consider) communication skills. It may vary from role to role, but it will be enough to potentially alter the candidates considered across the board. The best employees in your organization will, from the top down, understand and help convey the messages you need delivered, and the authorities on communication that you hire and allow to take lead will use their positions to strategically and proactively control the conversation.

As we'll see later in the book, not only is the strategic navigation of the public conversation crucial to surviving a crisis but it's also a key component to withstanding the scrutiny that can accompany a merger or litigation. Just as we saw in this chapter's example, by failing to have a culture that values communication skills, such that the management team was unable to look to a communications authority at the onset of its crisis, our fictional company was behind the story from day one. Whether the crisis is of greater or lesser severity, concerns rumors and unsubstantiated reports swirling around a merger, or results from the aggressive narrative of a litigious opponent, the only way to get ahead of the story is to have a team in place to proactively promote a narrative that is consistent with values the company's past behavior can support. The alternative is to scramble and react to the talking points of the last news cycle. In the next chapter, we'll use a communications audit to both better arm that team with the understanding and messaging they'll need to control the conversation, as well as put in place preparations long before the spotlight is on, which will give their message a believable place as part of the larger story that management wants told.

8

The Communications Audit

We've made arguments throughout this book to the effect that the fundamental problems plaguing modern companies unfortunately won't reveal themselves until a crisis or other attention-grabbing event unfolds. In walking through a company of our own creation, we were able to illustrate where some generic cracks in the foundation could be spotted and how they would leave the company vulnerable. Now it's time to take a look at steps that could be taken to prevent a crisis from becoming a catastrophe. In this chapter, we will discuss the communications audit as a process by which not only will the senior management team be made aware of the pitfalls potentially awaiting them but also will be immediately brought on board with the derived solutions. We will also look at the preparations for a potential storm, which a thorough communications audit conducted during more peaceful times can allow for.

When a distressing event—such as a litigation, crisis, or restructuring—hits your company, it is best that a completed communications audit is already available, with boardroom buy-in. It serves as a guideline for managing a distressed situation. But in the likely scenario that a communications audit has not been done ahead of time, the initial steps can still be completed to better manage the situation. The difference between "better manage" and "best manage" is why I always recommend conducting a communications audit with senior management that will prepare a company to respond to a distressed situation before it occurs. It is here that the boardroom will serve as the key component for the communications strategy.

The crucial components of a communications audit are: it is rigorous, based in data, and allows for effective intelligence gathering. All members of senior management and the board must have strong buy-in regarding how the corporation will respond once a situation occurs. However, one of the board members in the audit has to take a leadership role in forwarding this public relations agenda to the rest of the "influencers" in the corporation. As Irving Janis stated in reference to Kennedy:

> This proposed practice, which could not be instituted unless it were wholeheartedly approved, initiated, and reinforced by the President and other top executives in the hierarchy, can help to counteract the spontaneous group pressures for concurrence-seeking. It should certainly prevent an illusion of unanimity from bolstering a premature consensus.

At Silver Public Relations, we have been creating and using proprietary communications audits for 20 years. The questions we ask are drivers toward fact-based intelligence gathering that is truthful, objective, and effective in persuading the boardroom on the necessity to eliminate groupthink in formulating responses.

The public relations professional must start the internal audit with the CEO, then with the CFO and the human resources professional, and finally with the general counsel of the corporation. It is here that the right executives will be chosen for interviews and position statements will begin to be created that would eventually go to the media. Executives will be interviewed on all aspects of the "crisis," how it started, what had been done in the past to confront it, and how it will be resolved. All members of the board of directors will then be interviewed—with the understanding that not responding, or responding in a hurried fashion without preparation, is foolish and will hurt the company's reputation.

Even in an unfolding crisis, a company can get a better handle on the situation if the initial steps of the communications audit are completed. This is the intelligence-gathering phase and can be done quickly. At this point, key messages to be used in interviews and position statements are developed. If the issue is already in litigation, there is information that cannot be communicated, and working with the general counsel and outside lawyers will help craft that aspect of the case.

The most important part of the communications audit is to educate the boardroom to facilitate a buy-in on the cause that will create a positive effect. There will be little groupthink once this process is completed. The end result is a successful communication of messages that will help your company's side be weighed fairly in the court of public opinion.

THE COMMUNICATIONS AUDIT IN ACTION

A communications audit provides senior management with the tools and intelligence that allow a company to deliver messages that resonate when they most need to. The problem leading in to a process like this is that more often than not, senior management has had its fill of "silver bullet" ideas and power tools, which were supposed to have already made a difference. What makes the audit different, and what helps ensure both its acceptance and its effectiveness, is that it includes the senior executives from the beginning.

Buy-in

When I conduct an audit, I sit down with the senior team and let them audit themselves. I lead them in discussions and have them start by simply telling me about the company. What I'm looking for isn't the good things—I know the good things already; what I want is for them to tell me about the potential crises, so I start the conversation with something like the following:

- "Tell me where things can go wrong."
- "Are competitors spreading bad rumors about you?"
- "Are your numbers not really what they should be when you're reporting them?"
- "Do you have any potential losses coming against you either internally by employees or anywhere else?"

A number of things are happening simultaneously in this conversation. With the information I'm given, I can begin to design a strategy for how to deal with problems before they happen. In listening to the team articulate their weaknesses, I also get my first taste of who among them has the potential communication skills to speak before a larger audience, should it be necessary, and whose exposure we might need to limit (or to riff on the old adage: who has a face for radio and a voice for print). Most important, by laying their cards on the table, senior management has both owned up to its problems and started along on the path toward buy-in for a solution.

Imagine this same conversation with an internal VP, called in to speak with her superiors. Would he get the same level of honesty and self-reflection? More important, would his proposals be treated as if they were coming from an authority? Of course not: his ideas would be from a subordinate; if he were an authority, he would have been in the room before the conversation started. That is the advantage of bringing in an outside auditor: it brings immediate credibility to the subject. It also represents one of the goals of the process—to make sure that at its conclusion, there is a recognized communications authority on the senior management team because the value of such a person has been directly illustrated.

Transparency

Buy-in also comes from transparency. We discussed earlier the likelihood that entering a communications audit wasn't a prioritized need for most companies. What absolutely cannot happen during an audit is for the auditor to come on board, snoop around, and then deliver a series of recommendations that have no context for senior management. While I've already mentioned that the ideal time to bring in an auditor is long before a company is under the microscope, more often than not, I'm called in as things are already starting to heat up. As a result, I spend a lot of my time dealing with management teams focused on one single objective—get rid of the crisis. It's up to me to include them in the process, so they understand what I'm doing and where my recommendations are coming from; otherwise, there is a greater likelihood that when I step out of the room, I create an authority vacuum in communications. In the absence of a communications authority, groupthink takes over.

Transparency is as much about buy-in as it is about education. While in hindsight the media responses from the companies in crisis that have been profiled in this book can seem incompetent to many, we know that a lack of perspective did the most to set each company up for failure. As we saw in the previous chapter, that lack of perspective regarding communication skills is endemic at every level of the organization and rampant among senior management teams. As the communications audit progresses, some of the original assertions made in the boardroom will be challenged by findings uncovered elsewhere in the company. When these discrepancies are brought to light, and the strategy for dealing with the crisis as a whole evolves, management is given the opportunity to see how communication failure at the internal micro-level could contribute to a massive failure on a macro-level. In getting to the truth of the problem at hand, the auditor demonstrates the value of the steps they've taken, further ensuring buy-in to the recommendations that will follow. The auditor's internal investigation—when thorough—will make it clear to all of the major stakeholders: what needs to be done now, what the potential next crisis will be if not dealt with immediately, and what the best process is for finding and dealing with these matters.

Once it's clear what the message needs to be and who the target audience is, the next step will be to determine who is the best person to deliver the message and what outlets will be most receptive toward it. As noted earlier, in my role as an auditor, to some degree I've been looking for a spokesperson from my first meeting with management. I've made preliminary evaluations of their communication skills during all of our interactions, and—now that I know what my message is—it's time to fine-tune the conversation I want to take place around it. So if it's a technical issue, let's get the chief technology officer out there; if it's a financial issue, let's get the CFO. If it's an issue where the CEO would seem like an appropriate source, but the truth is that she's not a good speaker, then perhaps we'll need to find an appropriate substitute. Is there another team member who can step in, is there time for media training, and will our prospective speaker take to it? Finding the best messenger is still only half the battle; now it's time to look outside the organization and pick the best medium for our message.

External Audit

Think back to our discussion of communications history and the Shannon-Weaver model, which served as the foundation for most of Chapter 5.

Our message originates with a source of our choosing, and we've taken extra effort to ensure we've got the most effective source available in this case. It needs to reach a target destination, which can range from an angry twitter-sphere on the brink of outrage and requiring pacification to a group of concerned investors ready to bail out of your stock (or both at the same time). Between them is a transmitter and its receiver, along with whatever noises the former may burden on the latter.

The external audit is the process by which the communications auditor will choose the most effective transmitter/receiver

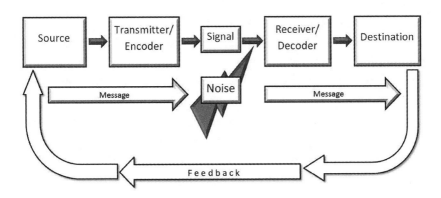

pair for delivering the strategically constructed message intact. This involves research across multiple outlets and varied media. The auditor looks back to situations similar to what the company is currently facing and finds which journalists have covered it and from there, what kind of slant they have. If a journalist (transmitter) or an outlet as a whole (receiver) has shown a particular slant over and over, that's the noise that will distort your message as it is being relayed, impacting the destination audience in a way that will cause more damage than good. Key to the communications strategy is determining which "transmitters" will be favorable, which will be fair, and which receivers will broadcast to a large enough audience to have an impact.

Regardless of whether they're engaging in an audit, managing a crisis, or just conducting day-to-day business, communication specialists rely on their contacts in the media to help them navigate through these decisions. Knowing who can and can't be trusted, who will be fair, and who means well but is overruled by editors or ownership makes the difference between an averted crisis and a story that won't go away. If it's clear to me that a volatile journalist from a newspaper with a considerable reach is going to come after the company I represent, then it's up to me to find an outlet of greater reach and grant it access to my source first. In a perfect world, my bigger and better outlet has slanted favorably toward companies like mine in the past, but—if that's not what's available—as long as they've proven themselves to be fair, it will get the message I want delivered in a way that will devalue opposing pieces with less information. From my own experience going into the situation, together with everything I've learned through the audit, I can create a pecking order to determine which print, which online, and which television outlets get my message first and in the process, help create the influencers that will push the narrative our internal audit determined would best address the situation.

Similarly, if our imaginary CEO isn't a good speaker, but I feel that she's an essential component to our message, then finding the best medium becomes an exercise in finding an outlet that plays to her strengths and allowing others to pick up the slack elsewhere. I may not make her available for live interviews, but I will have her author a statement instead.

This is how strategic and effective communication works. If the corporate response to a potential crisis is to avoid comment, then the only story told will be the one targeting your company. By determining the best message, the clearest source, and the most effective transmitters, we've not only given ourselves the best chance to communicate directly with our targeted audience without noise, but we're also reaching an equally important secondary audience—the media itself. Not every journalist is out to get you; not every blogger will carry your message *verbatim*; but if the lead story on your company holds up, if your investigation inside the company has resulted in a truthful account that incorporates the solution into the problem—and that's the story being told—then more often than not, others within the media will follow the lead of what came first. The influencers in the media not only influence the public but also influence everyone else in the media, and it's your job to make sure that the story they tell first—the message that leads the conversation—is the one you want them to tell.

CREATING A BETTER TRUTH

In every discussion of the communications audit throughout this book, we've mentioned how essential it is that it produces an honest appraisal of the company's strengths and weaknesses. I believe it's safe to assume that the best way to defend yourself from an attack is to know your weaknesses ahead of time. For a corporation, this means using the audit to make changes and enact policies and initiatives that can be used later on to support the transparent communication required during a crisis.

While the child who cleans his room the night before parent-teacher conferences might have his motives called into question, the company that can spend a few years building its reputation through community outreach and cause-based marketing, with a consistent message promoting the same, might be earning itself the benefit of the doubt when times get tough. Whether it was by this process or not, Apple was able to successfully leverage its reputation for quality against accusations suggesting otherwise. By all means, Toyota should have done the same, which makes their inclusion as a case study to be avoided so frustrating.

The strengths and weaknesses discovered during an audit are what your communications team will be fortifying or building on during quieter times, which creates for them a story worth telling when the stakes are raised. That being said, what if the greatest weakness discovered is not in the books or with business operations, but a deficiency with the team itself? The unifying elements that will allow a restructured organization to function properly, buying in to communication-driven decisions, and avoiding groupthink while leading up to those decisions, are the critical abilities of its management team—and the values that the company as a whole places on critical skills. In the next chapter, we will address what I feel to be one of the greatest disservices committed by our higher education system—the misplaced values it has produced—and how to institute the sea change necessary to correct it.

9

Reeducating Corporate America

As discussed earlier, executives of corporations tend to be well educated, and they tend to come from backgrounds in finance. Usually, they have excelled in running divisions and producing product lines that have contributed to the company's bottom line. If they are successful, they have expanded the market share of their products or services. Traditionally, they have studied all the best models for running a company, but the value of a chief executive who really understands corporate communications cannot be underestimated. Most executives in American companies are not prepared to shoulder communications responsibilities because their education did not prepare them for this function. The result of this is that corporate communications is relegated to a communications or marketing department. It is supposed to drive the firm's reputation from a distance, away from the central decision makers and leadership. But as communication is downplayed in the C-Suite until it is desperately needed, by then it may well be too late. The C-Suite is isolated from the whole subject until a crisis unfolds. This is a major structural flaw in many corporations.

Once we accept that financial public relations must communicate a corporation's image and message in order to help it survive in a complex business environment, then the only solution necessitates strong media training for executives in the C-Suite as well as the public relations department down the hallway from the boardroom. Both the executives in the boardroom and the communications executives need to understand effective strategies and tactics if they're ever going to be able to speak the same language. The need for executive leadership classes and training to integrate communications into a program that includes finance, accounting, negotiations, IT, and management cannot be overemphasized. If the executives in the C-Suite are to develop effective strategies and tactics, be able to anticipate crises, and keep a strong positive image for a corporation's brand—whether we're talking products, or services, or both—communications must be stirred into the brew.

CRITICAL DECLINE

A few years back, a friend of mine was teaching a graduate-level class in communications and invited me in as a guest lecturer. Before me, I had around 25 students, half of whom were from China, Latin America, or Europe. I presented various case studies to the class, and in the discussion following each, I began to notice that only the foreign students were engaging in any sort of critical thinking. As smart as they were, the American students would only regurgitate facts back to me, while the Chinese, European, and Brazilian students were much more likely to address the topic with a critical analysis of the underlying causes that contributed to it.

When the class was over, my friend and I discussed what had transpired. She confirmed for me that the Americans were mostly honor students, all had maintained high GPAs during their undergraduate studies and scored well on their GMATs, yet they still tended to be more likely to misread given scenarios and submit papers littered with mistakes. As much as this was a small sample, it reflected what I see and worry about when it comes to American workers and executives in companies across the country and around the globe. Not only are their international counterparts coming to the table with the benefits of a high school education that is measurably superior, but they also have a significantly greater grasp of communication basics. The informal assessment of the American graduate students I encountered, as compared to their foreign peers, was that their basic writing skills didn't hold up. Even in a nonnative language, the international students were routinely constructing better arguments with better grammar.

The Humanities

After having spent four years in a Ph.D. program in History at UCLA, I decided that I did not want to focus on academic research and writing, I wanted to learn serious nonfiction writing. I then went to graduate school at USC and studied journalism at the Annenberg School, and the basic rule was: when trying to reach a mass audience, you needed to write at about a seventh grade level. What I've seen since then is that more often than not, the business school audience is at or below the level of the masses. Despite their obvious intelligence, their advanced management training, and their abilities in dealing with numbers— whether in finance or accounting—they transmit and receive communications as if they weren't even in middle school.

How did this happen? How is it that a growing number of the most brilliant people who come out of business school— the executives and leaders of tomorrow—don't understand basic

119

grammar? It wasn't always the case. This isn't about intelligence or work ethic, nor is it another indictment of public schools or students "left behind"—remember, we're talking about top-level graduate students.

Anecdotally, I believe that we've steered away from a fundamental building block of what it once meant to be educated. In an age flooded with text, it is my observation that as a whole, we don't read as much as we used to. I don't have a comprehensive study of American reading habits to support my statement, but as far as trends go among the business circles I've run in, I've noticed a marked decline of colleagues who regularly engage in long-form reading. Perhaps the onslaught of modern distractions has taken a toll on our collective attention spans; or, in the abundance of posts on the Internet, we're experiencing a dearth of quality writing and have conditioned ourselves to stay clear of longer articles—never mind book-length works.

While my theories on reading are more personal musings than defensible positions, a limited reading capacity within the managerial ranks of corporate America does correlate to a shift in academic programs—which have in turn, influenced hiring. A 2013 Sunday opinion piece in the *New York Times*, lamenting the decline of the English major, prompted responses from several different outlets. Verlyn Klinkenborg wrote the article, and—having taught nonfiction writing at both the undergraduate and graduate levels at several prestigious universities, including Harvard, Yale, and Columbia's Graduate School of Journalism—Klinkenborg cites the drop in Yale BA graduates with English degrees by over 60% annually, from 1991 through 2012, as the centerpiece to his position. Ultimately, Klinkenborg argues that the specialization, which once defined graduate level programs, has now crept into undergraduate study, and the ambiguous career applications of English and other humanities-based degrees is steering students away from those tracks.

Nate Silver, whose statistical analyses brought him to national prominence during the 2010 and 2012 election cycles, responded to the Klinkenborg article in his *New York Times* blog. Silver's research illustrated a drop in English degrees, as compared to all bachelor's degrees awarded, by about 3.5% from 1971 to present day (although the numbers are a little flatter when he factored in the rise in the total number of students). Other degree tracks remained more or less stable, with slight percentage drops for math and engineering, and the largest losses in the social sciences—at about 8%. In their stead were rises in more career-oriented programs, including health (5.5%) and business professions. Silver showed that 7.5% more undergraduates are taking home degrees in business than they were 40 years ago, and with that rise, over 21% of all bachelor's degrees are now going to business majors. As a result, we have more business school students whose entire post-secondary academic paths have been entirely one dimensional, and a regular MBA crop insufficiently prepared to think and communicate critically once they enter the workplace.

In the short term, the logic would seem to make sense for an 18-year-old student. Why commit to a course of study that for many will be tied to significant student loan debt, which will literally take them a lifetime to pay back (at least the one lived thus far), if it does not logically tie in to a career track? The health services sector is seen by many to be bountiful with job opportunities for the generation to come, and if those with a head start in terms of academic preparation have the best chance of making it further, then many a major will be decided on that line of thinking. What exactly can a humanities degree—whether in English or anthropology—or a major in any of the natural sciences, contribute to a business education?

To start, lets erase the over-simplified notion of humanities study as beginning and ending with a pile of books written by dead European authors, with some early 20th-century Americans sprinkled on top for modernity's sake. The concept of the canon, in literature and other fields, has evolved from the reading list that sparked discussion of theme and motif in high school English classes to the heart of the discussion itself—namely, what is worthy of study, what has been omitted, and why? Ask a group of friends or coworkers to rate the most important movies, television shows, or ballplayers, and you'll wind up with a light discussion seasoned with a lot of head nods and general agreement. Ask the same question to a group of humanities scholars, and you might need to put on a pot of coffee. Positions will be staked out, arguments will follow, and the undeclared winner will be whoever comes to the fight with the most relevant facts, the most effective rhetorical or writing style, and the sharpest critical skills. Humanities scholars will debate in this fashion because it is exactly what they were trained to do—to study and read the world around them through analysis and criticism.

Small business expert Steve Strauss responded to Klinkenborg's piece with a *Huffington Post* article entitled, "Why I Hire English Majors." As an entrepreneur, Strauss recognizes the boldness in choosing an English degree, and praises the critical thinking experience these scholars bring to the table:

> They know how to think, to think for themselves, and how to analyze a problem. Business majors are fine, but they are preoccupied with theory, proving themselves, and doing it "right." But the English majors are used to getting a tough assignment, figuring it out, and getting it done . . . English majors are interesting, well spoken, can take a position and defend it with logic and reason . . .

Strauss isn't alone in his assessment; Earl Feldhorn is senior vice president at Wedbush Securities, one of the largest brokerage and investment banking firms based in Los Angeles. A legend in the field, he has been with the firm since the early 1960s and, when he and I discussed hiring college graduates, he told me "When I look for a graduate now, I'd rather they study English literature or the humanities because just knowing numbers, statistics, and finance is not enough. I want them to study communications, be able to think widely and critically, *and* be able to write. Few of these graduates know how to write or communicate, and that is a problem on Wall Street."

What these leaders are recognizing, and what I've been advocating all along, is that—at both the basic skills level and in the bigger picture—there is a deficiency in the pure business study track. If the thinking on the student's part is, "I want to get a job and make money," followed by "there's money to be made in business and therefore that's what I'll study," what's being left out of the equation is what sets many of the great leaders apart and determines not only whether the right idea can be communicated when it's needed most but also whether the person with that idea has the conviction to fight for it.

The solution here isn't to walk along a university quad and make the first kid you see reading David Halberstam, Mark Twain, Peter Drucker, Ernest Hemingway, F. Scott Fitzgerald and Charles Dickens your next CEO (a task made much more difficult in the age of e-readers). Rather, it is to seek out and value—at every step—those whose education and experience goes beyond the same theories of business and management that every other candidate seems to have ingested *verbatim*. Those theories have their place, but they are much more powerful in the hands of a leader who can wield them with critical precision and communicate their findings with similar effectiveness— knowing when they need to be followed, when they must be adapted, and when the best option is to discard them entirely and blaze a new trail. The final option—blazing a new trail—is certainly the scariest for management to consider—especially during a crisis—but if out-of-the-box thinking is the only way out of a bad situation, then it must be recognized that the road to innovation can only be cleared by those equipped with the tools to move forward.

Continuing Education

If you accept the argument that we have limited the scope of available experience within our workforce by overvaluing early academic specialization, it still doesn't change the company you're keeping. If you studied business at every step of your academic life, from your first lemonade stand to your MBA, has your fate already been sealed? Of course not. John Wooden, one of the most successful coaches of all time, whose thoughts on basketball and leadership transcended the game and inspired millions toward countless other pursuits, was fond of saying, "It's what you learn after you know it all that counts." Well, here's your chance.

My perspective on how we should revolutionize American business and reclaim the skills we've left behind has clear influences. In my twenties, I pursued a Ph.D. in history, and it was my scholastic training toward this degree that led to my own critical thinking on business. From my reading of Halberstam's *The Best and The Brightest*, I recognized the specter of groupthink regularly pushing itself into the bad decisions I repeatedly saw let loose by corporate decision makers—echoes of the Cuban missile crisis reverberating off of executive suites across the country. In studying public relations, I saw how the failure of the communication model led to the conditions in which groupthink flourished.

What my background in history led me to realize was that this was not the first time, as a nation, we've come to a roadblock created by our own insufficient communication skills. At the start of the 20th century, we were pretty illiterate on the national level. We were a society of working class immigrants literally building this country but lacking the means to advance our culture from the heights of our physical accomplishments. It wasn't until the early teens that the U.S. government put mandates in place that pretty much required every child to attend school until the 12th grade.

The effect, on both the first generation of U.S. children attending public school and on their parents, was a more educated society that could read, write, and practice basic math skills. They were better able to function in a civilized society and better understand what it means to live in a democracy. This was a cultural sea change, basic in its approach but radical enough to fundamentally improve the lives of generations to follow, and it's right in line with what I'm proposing now.

To better function in a 21st-century society and understand what it means to live in a world heavily influenced by global communication and social media, we need to reeducate ourselves. I've already argued for the equivalent of mandatory education for the next generation of business leaders in the form of a greater appreciation for the humanities, but for their "parents"—current professionals and leaders—a proactive approach is required. It isn't enough for today's managers to learn new skills by making solid hires and trying to figure out what they already know: that's a recipe for either losing good workers to competitors who already understand their value, or worse—becoming obsolete. To thrive in the modern environment, every professional must make continuing education a part of his or her own career path.

I latched onto the concept of continuing education while taking classes toward an executive MBA at The Drucker School of Management at Claremont Graduate University. A number of things about the Drucker approach impressed me. It directly influenced much of my thinking on communication failure in the boardroom and across companies as a whole, and did so by setting itself apart from other schools. I saw at Drucker an emphasis on communication and ethics that I found to be totally absent from other programs (it took the Enron scandal to really bring ethics into the classroom at other universities). Not only did they teach communications, when it wasn't even a part of the framework elsewhere, but they specifically taught the executives how to practice communication in a distressed situation as more than a mere exercise in propaganda.

This teaching was truly ahead of its time—a part of the Drucker system going back to the 1940s—but the business establishment, along with rival academic programs, generally looked down upon it at first. Eventually, mass communication began to branch out beyond network coverage and regional newspapers, and then the advent of social media followed, giving the world a way to amplify collective opinions. It meant that those who saw through the propaganda suddenly had the means to shine a light on it for everyone else, and those who knew how to communicate effectively were positioned to survive. When Drucker died in 2005, he was honored around the world and regarded as both a brilliant thinker and "the Father of Modern Management." His death was covered on the covers of *Time* and *BusinessWeek*.

One of the key elements of Drucker's brilliance is that—even before the communications skills gap was so apparent—he recognized business leaders did not always come into their positions fully formed. Opportunity, family, hard work, and good old fashioned luck may have all played a part in getting you there, but Drucker firmly believed in continuing education as a method of supplementing those existing traits to take a leader to the next level. He once said, "Knowledge has to be improved, challenged, and increased constantly, or it vanishes," and his belief was that even after you leave the university, you never stop learning because if you did, you were foolish.

Ultimately, that's the takeaway from this chapter. From the corporate boardroom to the last entry-level employee, continuing education must become the best-recognized path for career development. Regardless of your title, you have a responsibility to yourself and the company you work for to foster the skills required in the modern world. The first step in doing so is postgraduate education in the form of Master classes on the fundamentals of communication. Specifically, that means taking courses in writing, grammar, and the humanities, or even single intensive seminars in communications, to better prepare yourself and your staff for the challenges ahead. For those who do excel in communications, the PR professionals who may find themselves looked upon with greater appreciation in a setting where everyone understands the value of what they do, their challenge is to fill the gaps in their own education. It is in the best interest of communication professionals at every level to continue their own education by taking classes in accounting, economics, and finance so that they might better understand what's driving the other stakeholders in a given situation.

In Walter Isaacson's magisterial book *Steve Jobs*, he quotes Jobs saying that "I always thought of myself as a humanities person as a kid, but I liked electronics. Then I read something that one of my heroes, Edwin Land of Polaroid, said about the importance of people who could stand at the intersection of humanities and science, and that's what I wanted to do." Jobs became a master at integrating humanities, science, and business. That is why he was so successful. I would argue that his love of humanities as a child, while incorporating electronics and business as he got older, was the underlying reason for his success at Apple.

A NEW WORLD

In the spring of 2013, I was interviewed for an article for one of Ernst & Young's (E&Y) magazines. The reporter who contacted me did so because, from E&Y's London offices, he was beginning to recognize a trend in which E&Y clients were fearful over the effects of groupthink on their organizations and their investments. Like me, he saw communication failure as a primary cause and believed the only way to combat it was education. As more articles like this find their way to publication, it represents a significant step in the evolution of the business community's thinking on communication fundamentals as a necessary component of success, either as a component of undergraduate study or through continuing postgraduate education.

Recently, I was approached to bring my understanding of effective communication directly to business leaders at a global level. Valiant Business Media, a consulting group, has hired me to teach Master classes to executives from oil and energy companies who want to learn what they believe business school failed to teach them. Beginning in 2014, I have classes scheduled in London and Houston, and I believe that Valiant has committed to offer these classes because they've picked up on similar concerns about groupthink and the level of corporate discourse in business today. That their recognition of the problem has been matched by an audience willing to subscribe to the solution I've outlined here should be an indicator that the time for action is now.

Courses grounded in the fundamentals or those, like mine, that are more situation-specific are vital to the success of the individual and the company. For senior management, they represent a lifeline, connecting their business acumen to the global stage upon which their work may be judged. Ultimately, they are the tools that will bring about the sea change I am prescribing and remake corporate America. A management team that is improving itself through continuing education and making communications a primary focus will experience a shift in how they appraise the professional world. Much to their detriment, what those who lack fully developed communication skills don't grasp is the degree to which they are judged for their missteps. Once proper grammar and syntax is seen, it can't be unseen; and by taking the time to learn the fundamentals, we will expect to see the same when we correspond with others.

Once expectations have been raised, then we will begin to see communication skills valued in every department of every company. This is how you change a business's culture. Earlier in this chapter, I discussed the expectations Earl Feldhorn at Wedbush Securities had regarding communication skills. Mr. Feldhorn would have his junior-level employees write short essay recommendations on potential stocks purchases. He would instruct them to do the research and respond with a one-paragraph decision, defending whether they should or should not buy the stock in question. The objective was to have them think critically and articulate their thoughts in a concise, but effective, manner. This is continuing education—in practice and at its best. The junior staff were taught to be better writers and given a chance to impress management with their skills. Those who made a better impression had the best chance to advance. When you target a specific skill and advance those who show some degree of mastery in it, you are stacking the deck in favor of those traits you believe will have the biggest impact on your success and survival.

We aren't limiting the need for strong communicators to key staff or essential departments; our goals are improved external communication to the outside world as well as more reliable and effective internal communication. Current leaders can enhance their skill sets through continuing education, and enrich their staff through assignments that both develop and incentivize the values being embraced, but—for a full shift in values to take root—it must be recognized in every hiring decision.

Thoughts on hiring will bring us full circle within this chapter, as a greater consideration of humanities study can potentially open up your hiring pool to more critically skilled candidates. But if there's anything we've learned over a generation of communications decline, it's that a resume only tells a carefully cultivated portion of the larger story. To get the whole picture—to see where experience, knowledge, and critical skills converge—I advise those who are making hiring decisions to put their applicants to the test by having them write essays.

For all candidates in strong contention for positions in your company, have them each write a one-page essay (no more, no less) on what they believe their job description is. What you're looking for is one analytical page that showcases their abilities to demonstrate coherent thought. They can base their responses on the postings they applied to, the interviews they've taken part in, or their understandings of how a business unit functions, but they must articulate it in a relevant matter, in support of a central thesis and taken to a logical conclusion. In the process, they will demonstrate what they think about the job, how they communicate, what kind of writing skills they possess, and whether they are analytical thinkers. Right away, you'll be able to pick out which candidates broadly understand what the job entails and whether they are equipped to handle it. Those who are will represent the best options for organizational transformation, either as new leadership, reinforcements to the same, or foundations for the next generation.

10

Effective Communications for Litigation, Mergers, and Acquisitions

In Chapter 7, we created our own company to get a closer look at where and why breakdowns occur during crises and how groupthink takes hold. The argument was that at a time when the world is watching, having a communications authority in place provides senior management with the leadership they need to avoid making decisions based on self-interest or group dynamics. We have profiled companies that skillfully handled their crises, outlined the communications audit process, which highlights the areas of weakness within an organization, and labeled some of the traits to look for in a communications leader. Now is the time to put it all together, mindful of our discussion in Chapter 6 of the connection between public relations and investor relations.

In this chapter, we will again look at our fictitious company from Chapter 7. Here, we will pick up our corporate brainchild after its unfortunate social media meltdown and join up with it after its communications audit. We will then follow through some of the cultural transitions and departmental reorganization resulting from that audit and put our new communications team to work, just in time to face a gauntlet of internal and external challenges.

When we outlined the communications audit in Chapter 8, one of the key motivators for bringing on an external auditor was buy-in. In looking outside its own walls to fix the problem, senior management is positioning the auditor as an authority to be taken seriously. When the CEO, CFO, and general counsel, among others, all recognize that a problem exists and are all in agreement that an audit is necessary, they are also more likely to accept the recommendations made at the end of the process.

Now that our auditor has met with management and had the chance to develop conclusions concerning our situation, it will hopefully be possible to limit the damage by going on the offensive—determining the most appropriate message and then finding the best sources and most effective media to deliver it. We can theorize potential solutions here in the same way we could have piled onto the problem in Chapter 7, but—in a chapter that began by stating it was going to put all the pieces together—it would be no surprise to find that our exclusive profile done by a fair reporter at a rival news organization to our chief attacker did the job. Perhaps the more educational angle would be to accept that our auditor was able to get ahead of the story, and now to look ahead to other situations in which we would need communications to lead the way and benefit from the changes put in place following our audit.

LITIGATION

When you factor in the current corporate legal environment and the costs associated with litigation, in terms of both defense and actual liability, you can only come to one conclusion: lawsuits are neither a legal issue nor a communications issue—they are a corporate risk management issue. In California alone, this translates into 63% of companies increasing their legal spending by more than $1 million—before even getting to actual settlement costs. In the process, they are hiring outside law firms at a greater rate to cover the workload. Fortunately for our fictitious company, they've taken their original audit to heart after dealing with their media crisis. They've gone so far as to install a Chief Communications Officer (CCO) to control messaging internally, through the communications vice presidents for each unit, as well as to conduct and execute whatever strategies prove necessary during a crisis or litigation. This is all fortunate because our fictitious company is now getting sued.

Strategy

The same degree of auditing that got our company's house in order from a communications perspective is going to be required at a more specific level when it faces litigation. Just as before, it begins with intelligence gathering—here, a representative of our CCO and either general counsel or members of an outside firm may be working together upfront in the gathering of objective knowledge about the case. From the highest levels of authority to support staff and external sources closest to the lawsuit's target in day-to-day interactions, the feedback collected will provide a foundation for the media messaging and give the lawyers a critical analysis of the litigation PR landscape.

The crucial difference in our current scenario is that the communications audit may now either originate internally, with a communications authority figure already in place and on the senior management team, or use the improved internal structure to better work with an outside public relations firm. If an outside firm is needed, they now have a direct contact in senior management to work with and can freely communicate with whomever they need to under the protection of attorney-client privilege—extended between prospective defendants and public relations firms for litigation and investigation purposes.

Whether it's an in-house team or an outside firm, their job is to formulate a proactive and strategic campaign before, during, and after litigation. They will craft messages designed to gain a public opinion advantage and target specific audiences, among them: shareholders, institutional investors, the Securities and Exchange Commission and other regulatory agencies, company employees, vendors, analysts, boards of directors and the rest of senior management, and the media in general.

Communication Stages During Litigation

At different stages of the trial process, their objectives will change. Before the trial, the communications team will be actively battling to mitigate reputation risks, as opposing narratives will be submitted by their counterparts from rival PR teams, as well as the media itself. Our primary concern is that skewed and biased perspectives (intentionally crafted or otherwise) concerning our company not be allowed to take root and damage our reputation in the long term. At the same time, any shots at our company's reputation that are deflected, or messages that potentially help our cause, may also have value in influencing those directly responsible for the outcome of our case. Influencing juries may be a bit of a long shot, as far as strategies go, but judges are definitely counted among viable target audience members—a team that has done its homework and knows the thinking of certain judges, based on the decisions they've written, may incorporate elements resonant to that perspective within their messaging.

During a trial, the communication objectives will shift, as will the targets, to focus directly on clients, customers, and investors. At this stage, the message is one of translation; specifically, it is a repackaging of complex legal arguments and case milestones into a fair but sympathetic package that the designated audience can easily digest. For the audience we need to speak to at this stage, the best message is usually a story line that tells our side of things. The goal is to boil down the proceedings to the most essential facts that customers and investors need to understand so they may be inoculated to opposing perspectives, and to incorporate those facts into a narrative. If the story makes sense, the message is easier to accept.

When we tell our story to the public, we're also telling the individuals in the media who will rebroadcast it. This expands the scope of our target to not only reach individual stakeholders but also simultaneously influence the influencers, such that our company's take on what is happening is a part of the coverage of the case. Here, our team would directly reach out to reporters in the legal, business, and financial media, and also keep an updated pulse of the editors who serve as gatekeepers to key outlets. By offering up our own explanation of the events of the case as they unfold to reporters, we influence overall perception.

Throughout the proceedings, what you should never hear is that our company has "no comment" on a breaking aspect of the case, as "no comment" provides an opportunity for the opposition's narrative to take hold. Instead, by maintaining a consistent and logical message that explains our side of the case and the coverage of it, we can ensure that regardless of the verdict, our messages are read, heard, and understood. This will prove most important after the trial, as our PR group must now evaluate the effectiveness of the campaign and build on what they find to be the message that the public ultimately received, after being potentially distorted by the noise of bias and competing messages. Determining what our audience heard will be the first step in the next cycle of the process, factored in to new messaging that may be required, should we need to take efforts to restore our reputation or prepare for future litigation.

MERGERS AND ACQUISITIONS

Even though our "little company that could" has survived its brushes with out-of-control media-driven crises and held its reputation during a serious lawsuit, it isn't out of the woods yet. Perhaps the expenses and conditions surrounding these events were so costly that we are now facing bankruptcy and see a potential merger as an alternative; or, maybe we truly escaped unscathed and believe it to be the perfect time for a strategic acquisition to expand and improve our position. Either way, a key indicator of how successful we will be during our potential merger or acquisition is how our PR executives handle communications surrounding the deal.

Audience

As with the other examples we've explored, communications executives will work with the rest of senior management and outside firms—if necessary—to craft a messaging strategy. Audiences will be determined and targeted with what should be a clear and effective message explaining the complicated issues surrounding the deal. Similar to our audience during a legal defense, our PR team (or teams) will be focusing on outlets that reach out to: investors, customers, general counsel, boards of directors, foreign executives (if a global company), and also employees.

This last group should not be overlooked, as we've made considerable effort to incorporate employees with a greater appreciation of the communications discipline—with the understanding that our staff represents one of our greatest tools for word-of-mouth direct communication. Shoring them up with a message they can believe in is also a proactive measure against the potential damage of those who may use their own social networks or messaging boards to speak out of turn and potentially derail our communications efforts with a distracting message. Amazon is a company that I've always admired in this regard, as their expansion through acquisition has occasionally made them the target of criticism, yet their employees always seem to carry an evangelical belief in maintaining the company line and touting its progress.

Setting the Standard

Ultimately, by effectively reaching the groups we've targeted and getting them all on the same page, we create a cohesive message. When this is part of a strategy, it begins well before the deal is announced, so there is a foundation for the messaging to come—once the deal is made public and as it progresses. As opposed to a lawsuit or scandal, companies that initiate a merger or acquisition have a greater degree of control over the timing of the coverage. The ability to announce a deal prior to it leaking allows a company to influence the initial coverage of it in the media. In many ways, the first story on a deal is crucial, as it defines the debate to follow.

The stakes here can be significant, especially when the deal in question is a stock deal or subject to regulation, as either have the potential to drag out in the media and undergo more careful scrutiny. Shareholders left in the dark or misled by alarmist stories can be inclined to join together and challenge the deal or the price. Their concerns about the acquiring company must be alleviated. After all, if our company is making the acquisition, and it is our opinion that the deal will be profitable, then we need to make sure our story is out there. If our goals for the company are clear, and our history backs up our ability to execute them, that's a story that needs to be told, along with regular updates as the deal progresses.

Similarly, courts and regulators definitely keep an eye on the media. Should our deal be subject to the review or decision of either, we cannot go back in time to get the right facts in front of them; we need to have put them out from day one. If our deal is announced to the world as a leaked story that becomes part of a piece concerned with the implications of what's to follow, that will be the lens through which it is seen by many moving forward. Anyone with jurisdictional approval or influence over our ability to proceed will need to look things over with those concerns in mind and could potentially overcompensate in their findings to avoid accusations of impropriety. Just as bad, if shareholders' or regulators' initial impressions of our company are to see us on the defensive, we risk credibility and miss out on the opportunity to establish ourselves as trustworthy from the start. While the proactive efforts of our PR team could be challenged as the deal unfolds, the advantage they have—in their ability to set the standard for the coverage that follows by being open and transparent during its announcement—is one that cannot be squandered.

Conclusion

FROM GROUPTHINK TO GROUP DYNAMIC

As both a proactive and reactive strategy to dealing with distressed or tumultuous circumstances, effective communication works. It is your best option to demonstrate to the world that there is value in what you say, what you produce, and who you are as a company. For many of the people who buy your products, invest in your stock, or roam your halls from Monday through Friday—some staying after-hours to get the job done—what you communicate to them will be the beginning and end of what they know about your mission as a company. That is, until external forces become a factor.

More than anything, beyond the missteps and the groupthink, what the examples discussed in this book need to impress upon you is that the world is always changing, and you would be a fool to think otherwise. Messages change, circumstances change, media change, and you need to change with it. It doesn't matter what worked before, what got you to prominence, or how things used to be done. Doing business today as it was done even ten years ago would be like looking to Sterling, Cooper, & Partners from *Mad Men* to smoke and drink their way through your next million dollar advertising campaign.

It's not enough either to pay lip service to new concepts by being on Twitter or to have a Facebook page. Whatever influence either has, there will be something new to take its place soon enough—maybe a year from now, maybe less. Somewhere out there, the next influencing platform is being developed, and, when it comes around and some intern on your staff or a vice president's teenage kid visits the office and starts wondering why you're not reaching your audience there, your answer can't be "because we didn't know about it"—or worse, "because we don't understand it." What if, of all the tools in the new communications toolbox, it's Vine or Quora that somehow becomes the next site of controversy or opportunity for your company, and the person trying to make your management team understand what they need to do isn't already in position to influence them? What if the matter is urgent, as it has been in many of the examples we've explored, and the teams you have in place need to waste valuable time waiting on a debate they're not even a part of anymore, to conclude, or explain the particular online culture of where this battle is being staged to an out-of-touch management group, not even entirely convinced that such battles matter?

More than the newest wave of innovation and social media, change has also taken over the traditional channels. Is that full-page advertisement purchase going to influence anyone if no one's reading newspapers anymore? Maybe it's a part of a grander strategy, but the demands of that strategy are changing along with everything else, and now the best use of that advertisement may not be to target consumers, but to create such a bold statement that the media covering your industry—already reaching your target audience—will do it for you.

Being on top of the changes is as much a responsibility of management as knowing the latest regulations and current tax laws. The new ideal is an organization that can respond quickly to the world around it, whose communication teams are equipped to defuse a potential crisis and guide the press through the stages of a lawsuit or merger. It is this ideal that we've attempted to build throughout the preceding pages. By looking at the failures and successes that have come before us as examples, we can take away a greater understanding of the root of the problem and attempt to solve it.

Ideal circumstances begin with preparation. Any homeowner, who has ever purchased a snow blower in the summer, understands how important it is to have the necessary tools to deal with a situation on hand before a storm. Our argument has been straightforward in that the best preparation is education. The reintroduction of critical communication skills, reading, writing, and analytical thinking will open the door to better and more informed decisions and better leadership from every corner.

More than that, the type of education advocated in these pages is tied to a specific agenda in the remaking of corporate America—the devaluing and/or elimination of one-dimensional leaders and their progeny. Number crunchers are never going to be the source of true innovation. You cannot expect to thrive on accounting skills alone, just as you cannot expect to communicate effectively without some knowledge of what drives the numbers you're discussing. Our ideal organization needs to be looking for people who can demonstrate their abilities to both excel in their respective fields and to relate their knowledge to others.

At the same time as you're hiring a new wave of critical thinkers and readers, you need to look internally at your own abilities, and make the effort to improve upon whatever shortcomings you find—otherwise, you risk finding yourself grouped with all the ousted one-dimensional relics. Classes, seminars, and continuing education to equip yourself better for the challenges ahead are more available now than they ever were. Just because you work on the sales side of a web-based business doesn't mean you can't take a day for an HTML webinar, and just because you're responsible for coding the website of that same company doesn't mean you shouldn't be developing your own skills so that you can better communicate the technical problems you face to an internal audience that may not yet fully understand your skill set.

Eventually, there will be a familiar ring to all of this. Take stock in your skills, appraise your strengths and weaknesses, determine what message you're sending to your peers with action or inaction, and use your honest conclusions as a plan to move ahead. It's the same audit I've prescribed for the corporation, applied to the individual. And as your critical skills improve, the accuracy and usefulness of your internal audit will as well.

More than anything else, that's why I believe this is the approach that can lead us forward. It is a solution that improves its own foundation, upon which a better solution will be built. The pattern for company and employee—for the group as a whole and for each member within—is such that, once buy-in is achieved, it can feed itself on a path to overall improvement. The strength of the company is the individual, and the strength of each individual is being part of a company that will utilize his or her skills and value his or her contribution. This sounds simple—the sort of idealized HR statement that in the abstract anyone can get behind—but what we've seen in our discussion is that the one thing that repeatedly gets in the way and prevents the contributions from smart employees and talented leaders from being properly put to work is groupthink.

Effective communicators, who bring a critical approach to tackling the problems they face, don't get paralyzed: they speak their minds. These are the people you want working for you, working alongside you, and leading you. They exist in binary to every negative stereotype about corporate America: as free thinkers, instead of "yes men;" as leaders, instead of followers. I think for most people, this is who they imagined they'd become early on along their career paths, and what I'm saying is that at every level, communication skill is how you get there.

No one ever strived for mediocrity, hoped in business school that they'd one day work someplace average, or dreamed of barely surviving a corporate crisis that could have been prevented. So this is a call for change. By being able to express your ideas, you express your value. When you bring your value to a group discussion, you potentially balance out the values of others in a way that shows everyone that not only do options exist, but also that there is no damage in effectively voicing dissent. And when that dissent is backed by verifiable facts, is consistent with what the group you're speaking to already knows, and is presented in a transparent way that doesn't leave your audience suspecting an ulterior motive, you've delivered a message that people will listen to. If your entire organization is full of people who can do this, who can debate what's right and what's wrong from their perspectives, who can describe their big ideas and argue for them to be considered, who can defend pet projects and discourage that which wastes everyone's time, and who can deliver a message that not only finds its intended audience but also influences it, then the group as a whole can do the same thing. From there, effective communication can not only be achieved but also make a difference.

Communications groupthink in global corporations and organizations must be eliminated and this can begin to happen if there is more of an intersection between business classes and humanities in the education of upcoming leaders. As Peter Drucker wrote and stated in his books and classes, "management is a liberal art." He added that managers—who eventually become leaders—draw on all the knowledge and insights of the humanities and social sciences (psychology, philosophy, economics, history, ethics, etc.). When added to a rigorous study of accounting, finance, and other business classes, this should help mold future leaders; creating a corporate climate where group-think will become less of a factor in boardroom decision making during a restructuring, crisis, or litigation.

Bibliography

INTRODUCTION

Whyte, William H., Jr., "Groupthink," *Fortune*, March 1952.

Janis, Irving L., *Victims of Groupthink: A Psychological Study of Foreign-Policy Decisions and Fiascoes* (Boston: Houghton Mifflin, 1972).

Janis, Irving L., *Groupthink: Psychological Studies of Policy Decisions and Fiascoes of Foreign-Policy Decisions and Fiascoes* (Boston: Houghton Mifflin, 1982).

Halberstam, David, *The Best and the Brightest* (New York: Random House, 1972).

Bendery, Jennifer and Sabrina Siddiqui, "GOP Lawmakers Who Voted Against Iraq War Stand Their Ground 10 Years Later," *Huffington Post*, March 20, 2013 at: http://www.huffington post.com/2013/03/20/gop-iraq-war_n_2910618.html.

Brandt, Richard L., "Birth of a Salesman," *The Wall Street Journal*, October 15, 2011 at: http://online.wsj.com/article/SB10001424052970203914304576627102996831200.html.

CHAPTER 1

Crawley, John and David Lawder, "Probe Clears Toyota Electronics over Runaways," *Reuters*, February 8, 2011 at: ht

tp://www.reuters.com/article/2011/02/08/us-toyota-usa-id
USTRE7165SY20110208.

CHAPTER 2

Tapscott, Don and David Ticoll, *The Naked Corporation: How the Age of Transparency Will Revolutionize Business* (New York: Free Press, 2003).

CHAPTER 3

Bergin, Tom, "Analysis: BP PR Blunders Carry High Political Cost," *Reuters*, June 29, 2010 at: http://www .reuters.com/article/2010/06/29/us-oil-spill-bp-pr-idUSTRE 65S3JL20100629.

CHAPTER 4

"FedEx Guy Throwing My Computer Monitor," YouTube, December 19, 2011 at: http://www.youtube.com/ watch?v=PKUDTPbDhnA.

"'This won't be his best day:' FedEx vows to track down delivery man who tossed computer monitor over the fence," *The Daily Mail*, December 20, 2011 at: http:// www.dailymail.co.uk/news/article-2076432/FedEx-guy -caught-throwing-monitor-fence-YouTube-video.html.

"FedEx Response to Customer Video," YouTube, December 21, 2011 at: http://www.youtube.com/watch?v=4ESU_PcqI38.

Kelly, Tara, "FedEx Delivery Man Caught Throwing Computer Monitor Over Gate; Video Goes Viral (WATCH)," *The Huffington Post*, December 21, 2011 at: ht

tp://www.huffingtonpost.com/2011/12/21/fedex-delivery
-man_n_1162743.html.

Sebastian, Michael, "FedEx responds to simmering PR disaster caused by viral video," *Ragan's PR Daily*, December 22, 2011 at: http://www.prdaily.com/Main/Articles/10429.aspx.

JUSTICEFERGIE, "Papa John's Mitigates PR Disaster Using Twitter," *Babble.com*, January 8, 2012 at: http://www.babble .com/mom/papa-johns-mitigates-pr-disaster-using-twitter/.

"Taco Bell Meat: Chain Sued Over 35% Beef Content in 'Taco Meat Filling,'" *AP/Huffinton Post*, Jauary 24, 2011 at: http:// www.huffingtonpost.com/2011/01/25/taco-bell-beef -lawsuit_n_813185.html.

"'Thank You For Suing Us:' Taco Bell Fights Beef Lawsuit With Full-Page Ads," *AP/Huffington Post*, January 28, 2011 at: http:// www.huffingtonpost.com/2011/01/28/taco-bell-beef-meat -lawsuit-ads_n_815303.html.

Casey, Nicholas, "Brawl Over Doll is Heading to Trial," *The Wall Street Journal*, May 23, 2008 at: http://online.wsj.com/ article/SB120345433842377837.htm.

Zimmerman, Ann, "Bratz's MGA Alleges Mattel Spied on Rival Toy Makers," *The Wall Street Journal*, August 17, 2010 at: http://online.wsj.com/article/SB10001424052748704554 104575435832457778898.html.

Ionescu, Daniel, "Apple's iPhone 4 Antennagate Timeline," *PCWorld TechHive.com*, July 17, 2010 at: http://www.tech hive.com/article/201297/apples_iphone_4_antenna_gate_ timeline.html.

Gans, Joshua, "How Apple Broke the PR Rules—And Got Away With It," *Harvard Business Review, HBR Blog Network*, February 16, 2011 at: http://blogs.hbr.org/cs/2011/02/ how_apple_broke_the_pr_rules_a.html.

CHAPTER 5

Colvin, Geoff, "Secrets of Leadership from American Express: The Key to Ken Chenault's Plans for American Express: Industrial-Strength Candor," *Fortune*, September 19, 2007 at: http://money.cnn.com/2007/09/17/news/newsmakers/Ken _Chenault.fortune/.

Wiener, Norbert, *Cybernetics: Or the Control and Communication in the Animal and the Machine* (Paris: Hermann & Cie, 1948).

Shannon, Claude Elwood and Warren Weaver, *The Mathematical Theory of Communication* (Chicago: University of Illinois Press, 1949).

Thibault, John and Harold Kelly, *Social Psychology of Groups*, (New York: Wiley, 1959).

Hovland, Carl, Irving L. Janis, and Harold Kelly, *Communication and Persuasion: Psychological Studies of Opinion Change* (New Haven: Yale University Press, 1953).

Burke, Kenneth, *A Rhetoric of Motives* (Berkeley: University of California Press, 1969).

McLuhan, Marshall, *Understanding Media: The Extensions of Man* (New York: McGraw-Hill, 1964).

CHAPTER 6

Bernays, Edward, *Crystalizing Public Opinion* (New York: Boni and Liveright, 1923).

Lippman, Walter, *Public Opinion.* (New York: Harcourt, Brace, 1922).

Marchand, Roland, *Creating the Corporate Soul: The Rise of Public Relations and Corporate Imagery in American Big Business.* (Berkeley: University of California Press, 2001).

Tye, Larry, *The Father of Spin: Edward Bernays and the Birth of Public Relations*. (New York: Henry Holt and Company, LLC. 1998).

CHAPTER 8

Janis, Irving L., "Groupthink Among Policy Makers." Nevitt Sanford, Craig Comstock, et al., Sanctions for Evil: Sources of Social Destructiveness. (San Francisco: Josey-Bass, 1971).

CHAPTER 9

Klinkenborg, Verlyn, "The Decline and Fall of the English Major," *The New York Times*, June 22, 2013 at: http://www.nytimes.com/2013/06/23/opinion/sunday/the-decline-and-fall-of-the-english-major.html?_r=2.

Silver, Nate, "As More Attend College, Majors Become More Career-Focused," *The New York Times*, June 25, 2013 at: http://fivethirtyeight.blogs.nytimes.com/2013/06/25/as-more-attend-college-majors-become-more-career-focused/?smid=tw-fivethirtyeight&seid=auto&_r=0.

Strauss, Steve, "Why I Hire English Majors," *The Huffington Post*, June 23, 2013 at: http://www.huffingtonpost.com/steve-strauss/hiring-english-majors_b_3484409.html.

ESPN.com staff, "The Wizard's Wisdom: 'Woodenisms," June 4, 2010.

Drucker, Peter F. and Rick Wartzman, *The Drucker Lectures* (New York: McGraw-Hill Professional, 2010).

CONCLUSION

Isaacson, Walter, *Steve Jobs*, (New York: Simon & Schuster, 2011).

Appendix

GAP | Generally Accepted Practices

V 42312

GAP VII: Seventh Communication and Public Relations
Generally Accepted Practices Study (Q4 2011 data)

USCAnnenberg
School for Communication
and Journalism

*Strategic Communication
and Public Relations Center*

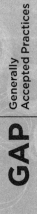

GAP | Generally Accepted Practices

USC Annenberg

About GAP

The purposes of the Communication and Public Relations Generally Accepted Practices (GAP) Studies, of which this is the seventh, are to provide practitioners with data they can use today to better manage the PR/Comm functions (PR/Comm) in their organizations; point out trends they must be aware of as they plan for tomorrow; and identify Best Practices against which they can benchmark their own organizations.

GAP provides insight into a variety of topics, such as:

Staff size, organization, functions, budgeting

Measurement and evaluation

Use of agencies

Client needs, perceptions

Relationship models

Compensation trends

154

GAP | Generally Accepted Practices

USC Annenberg

GAP VII Research Team

University of Southern California
Annenberg School for Communication and Journalism
Strategic Communication and Public Relations Center (SCPRC)

Jerry Swerling, M.A.
Director, PR Studies
Director SCPRC

Kjerstin Thorson, Ph.D.
Assistant Professor
Research Director SCPRC

Burghardt Tenderich, Ph.D.
Associate Professor
Associate Director SCPRC

In consultation with:

Niku Ward
Brenna Clairr O'Tierney
Mia Becker
Jessica Wang
Yueheng Li

David Michaelson, Ph.D.,
Managing Director, Teneo Strategy

Forrest Anderson, MBA, Independent
Communications Research and Strategy Consultant

M.A. Candidates 2013
Strategic Public
Relations, USC

GAP | Generally Accepted Practices

USC Annenberg

GAP VII Partners

GAP VII has been supported by these leading professional organizations:

The Arthur W. Page Society, the 400+ members of which are generally the heads of communication in major U.S. organizations

Institute for Public Relations (IPR), which serves as research partner, contributing its expertise in researching the science underlying the practice of communication

IABC International Association of Business Communicators (IABC), with its 15,000 member global network of communicators

Public Relations Society of America (PRSA) with its 21,000 members

GAP | Generally Accepted Practices

USCAnnenberg

About the USC Annenberg Strategic Communication and Public Relations Center (SCPRC)

The USC Annenberg Strategic Communication and Public Relations Center (SCPRC) plays a leading role in the continuing evolution and expansion of the public relations profession. Created by the Public Relations Studies Program of the USC Annenberg School for Communication and Journalism in 2002, the Center is one of the most ambitious efforts to date by a major American university to bridge the substantial gap between the public relations profession and the academic community that studies it.

The center's mission is to advance the study, practice and value of the public relations/communications function.

In an effort to bridge academia with the PR practice, the center conducts practical, applied research in areas such as best practices, program evaluation and emerging trends. In addition to informing practitioners, SCPRC's research results are being integrated into the USC Annenberg public relations curriculum.

USC Annenberg

GAP | Generally Accepted Practices

About GAP VII

GAP VII is the largest and most comprehensive study to date of senior-level PR/Comm practitioners in the United States. It was sampled from a comprehensive list of senior-level practitioners, each of whom received multiple invitations to participate. GAP VII is believed to be representative of the broad population of senior-level practitioners.

Accessing GAP VII

The GAP VII study is available for free download at www.annenberg.usc.edu/gapstudy.

More comprehensive and detailed findings are available in the GAP VII Insight Base at the same web address. This online catalogue contains information divided by private and public corporations of various sizes, as well as government agencies and non-profit organizations. It is designed for practitioners to access information specific to their own type of organizations.

For more information email scprc@usc.edu.

USC Annenberg

GAP | Generally
Accepted Practices

GAP VII Sample Methodology

GAP VII research was conducted in an online survey of top PR/Comm practitioners and data was collected in Q4 2011. GAP VII received more than 1,000 responses, and participants selected for inclusion had to pass a rigorous screening process to ensure that each respondent was the most senior communicator in the organization, or a direct report thereof. The final sample was 620.

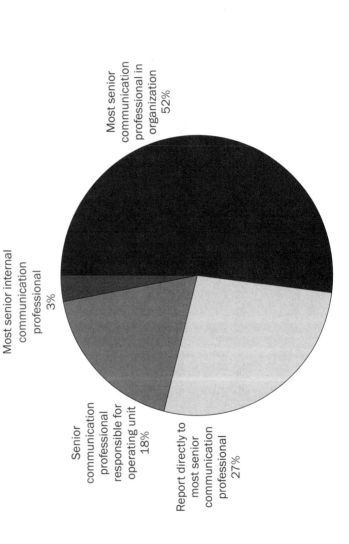

USCAnnenberg

GAP | Generally
Accepted Practices

GAP VII Respondents: Corporate, Government and Non-profit

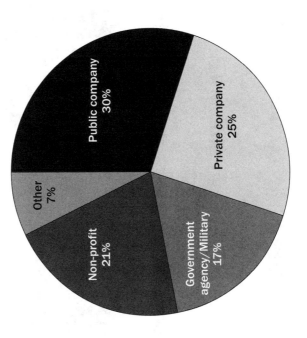

Public company
30%

Private company
25%

Government
agency/Military
17%

Non-profit
21%

Other
7%

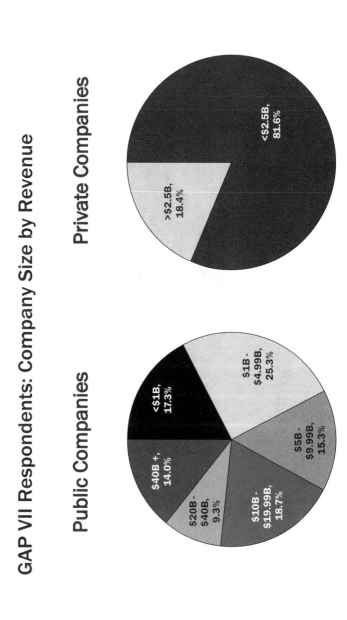

GAP | Generally Accepted Practices

USC Annenberg

GAP VII Respondents: Company Size by Revenue

Public Companies

Private Companies

GAP VII Respondents: U.S. and Multi-National Organizations

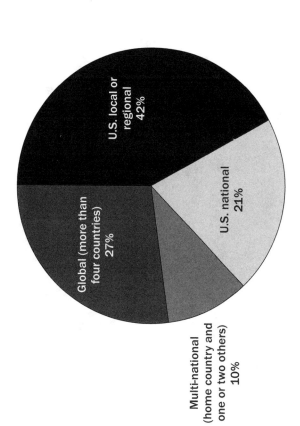

U.S. local or regional 42%

U.S. national 21%

Global (more than four countries) 27%

Multi-national (home country and one or two others) 10%

USC Annenberg

GAP | Generally Accepted Practices

All GAP VII Respondents: Academic Degrees

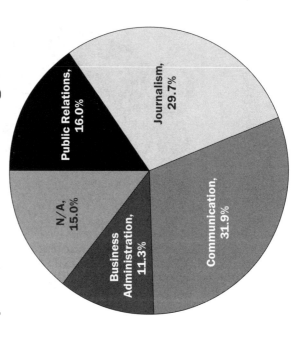

Public Relations, 16.0%

Journalism, 29.7%

N/A, 15.0%

Business Administration, 11.3%

Communication, 31.9%

More than 75% of respondents have an academic degree in either Journalism, PR or Communication

GAP | Generally
Accepted Practices

USCAnnenberg

Key Narratives

GAP VII offers insights on a variety of topics pertinent to the successful management of the public relations function:

1. Budgets
2. Functions/Responsibilities
3. Use of social media
4. Measurement and evaluation
5. Working with agencies
6. Organization/Reporting
7. C-Suite perceptions
8. Culture, character and integration
9. Excellence/Best practices

GAP VII, Section 1

Budgets

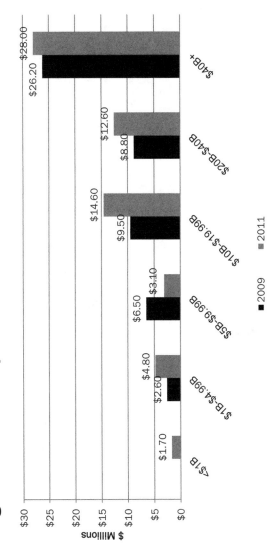

USC Annenberg

GAP | Generally Accepted Practices

Budgets: Public Companies, 2009 vs. 2011

Despite the difficult economic climate in the United States, public companies generally experienced an increase in their public relations budgets.

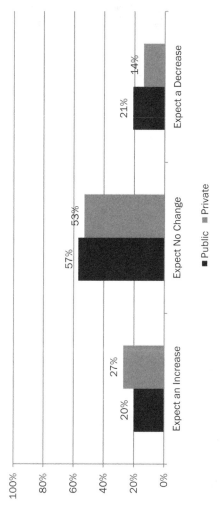

Budgets: Corporate Respondents, 2011 vs. 2012

More than 50% expect budgets to be flat in 2012, and more private than public companies expect a budget increase.

GAP | Generally Accepted Practices

USC Annenberg

Budget: Allocations

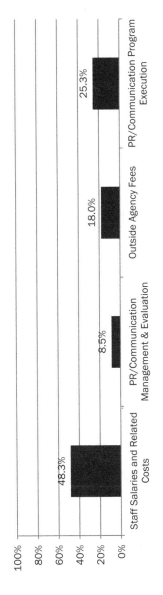

100%			
80%			
60%			
48.3%	8.5%	18.0%	25.3%
40%			
20%			
0%			
Staff Salaries and Related Costs	PR/Communication Management & Evaluation	Outside Agency Fees	PR/Communication Program Execution

Salaries and related costs account for almost 50% of budget, followed by Program Execution (25%), Agency Fees (18%) and Measurement & Evaluation.

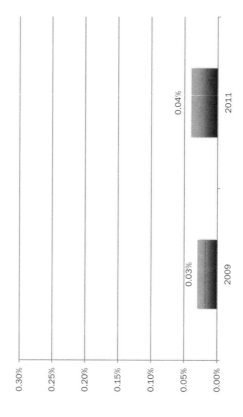

PR:GR Comparison, Large Public Companies, 2009 vs 2011

Among large public companies (20B+ revenue), the percentage of gross revenue (GR) spent on communication has increased over 2009.

GAP VII, Section 2

Functions and Responsibilities

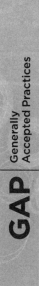

Core Budgetary Responsibilities

'Core' is defined as more than 50% of PR/Com departments report responsibility for this function in 2011.

	GAP 2009	GAP 2011
Corporate communication	87%	88%
Executive communications	74%	80%
Internal communications	67%	80%
Crisis management	73%	72%
Social media monitoring	53%	70%
Social media participation	53%	66%
Issues management	47%	58%
Community relations	56%	57%
Corporate external website	54%	55%
Corporate intranet	49%	54%
Marketing/Product PR	61%	50%

GAP Generally Accepted Practices

USC Annenberg

Budgetary Responsibilities in Corporations: On the Rise

Budgetary Responsibility	2009	2011	Increase
Social media monitoring & participation*	53%	70%, 66%	17%, 13%
Search engine optimization	18%	31%	13%
Internal communications	47%	58%	13%
Issues management	47%	58%	11%
Customer relations	6%	15%	9%
Multimedia production	new item	40%	—

*In 2011, monitoring and participation asked as two questions

As expected, social media monitoring and participation have significantly increased and can now be considered a mainstream responsibility of PR/Comm. Further reflecting a shift to Web 2.0 responsibilities is the rise of search engine optimization. Of particular interest is the significant increase in budgetary responsibility for customer relations, which might be in response to customers convening in social media.

GAP | Generally Accepted Practices

USCAnnenberg

Budgetary Responsibilities: On the Decline

Budgetary Responsibility	2009	2011	Decrease
Marketing/Product PR	61%	50%	-11%

Corporations report a significant decline in budget percentage allocated to marketing/product public relations.

GAP | Generally Accepted Practices

USCAnnenberg

Budgetary Responsibilities: Categories

Traditional	Digital	Advertising
Corporate communication	External website	Corporate
Executive communications	Social media monitoring	Product
Marketing/PR	Social media participate	
Crisis management	SEO	
Investor relations	Multimedia	
Community relations		
Issues management		
Standards		

Further analysis indicates corporate PR/Comm departments take on additional responsibilities—such as increased digital and social media activity—without an increase in budget.

GAP VII, Section 3

Use and Management of
Social Media

USC Annenberg

GAP | Generally Accepted Practices

Top 10 Digital/Social Tools (Corporate Respondents)

Social Networking Sites	4.75	Blogs	3.52
Sharing Online Videos	4.48	RSS	3.25
SEO	4.48	Tagging	3.00
Twitter	4.33	Co-creation of Content	2.83
Producing Online Videos	4.19	Online Audio	2.64

*1=Didn't use; 7=Used significantly

GAP Generally Accepted Practices

USCAnnenberg

Digital/Social Tools: On the Increase (Corporate Respondents)

Digital/Social Practice	2009	2011	Increase
Facebook	3.44	4.75	+1.31
Twitter	3.34	4.33	+.99
Blogs	2.72	3.52	+.80

*1=Didn't use; 7=Used significantly

178

USC Annenberg

GAP | Generally Accepted Practices

Digital/Social Tools: Core *

Digital/Social Practice	GAP 2009	GAP 2011
Social Networking Sites	3.44	4.75
Sharing Online Videos	4.32	4.48
SEO	NA	4.48
Twitter	3.34	4.33
Producing Online Videos	NA	4.19

1=Didn't use; 7=Used significantly

*Defined as above 4.0 average use

GAP | Generally Accepted Practices

USC Annenberg

Digital/Social Tools: On the Decline

Digital/Social Practice	2009	2011	Decrease
Wikis	1.96	1.80	-.16
Virtual Worlds (e.g., Second Life)	1.40	1.26	-.14

1=Didn't use; 7=Used significantly

Wikis and Virtual Worlds increasingly feel like early Web 2.0 tools that initially showed promise for PR/Comm, but continue to decline in use and relevance.

GAP | Generally Accepted Practices

USC Annenberg

Digital/Social Tools: Budgetary Control, Corporate Respondents

Department	70% Budgetary Control or Higher
PR/Communication	50%
Marketing	41%
Customer Service	6%
Information Systems	8%
Other	9%

Totals do not equal 100.

PR and Marketing are the most frequent "owners" of social media budgets. Half of corporate respondents report PR has more than 70% budgetary control of social media; 41% report Marketing has majority control.

GAP | Generally Accepted Practices

USC Annenberg

Digital/Social Tools: Strategic Control

Department	70% Strategic Control or Better
PR/Communication	54%
Marketing	37%
Customer Service	7%
Information Systems	7%
Other	11%

Totals do not equal 100.

Similarly, PR and Marketing are most frequently named as strategic "owners" of social media strategy.

GAP | Generally
Accepted Practices

USC Annenberg

Use of Mainstream Digital/Social Tools

Frequent users by organization type

36% of public companies

47% of private companies

40% of government agencies

66% of non-profits

Percentage of frequent usage among public companies

Twitter, 53%

Facebook, 53%

SEO, 52%

Blogs, 32%

RSS, 27%

Tag content, 25%

Mainstream digital/social media tools are adopted at various rates in different types of organizations. Two-thirds of non-profits report frequent use, compared to only 36% of public companies.

Among public companies, PR/Comm departments report the most frequent use of Twitter, Facebook and SEO.

*Scored above 4 on 7-point scale

GAP VII, Section 4

Measurement and Evaluation

GAP | Generally
Accepted Practices

USC Annenberg

Measurement and Evaluation:

As a top-level finding in GAP VII, budget allocated to measurement and evaluation by corporations is up substantially from previous studies:

9% (2011) vs. 4% (2009)

This pronounced rise speaks to the improved ability to measure web content via social media monitoring tools, but it may also indicate a more strategic view and use of public relations.

All findings in this section are specific to corporate use, while data for government agencies and non-profit organizations can be found online in the GAP VII Insight Base.

GAP | Generally Accepted Practices

USC Annenberg

Measurement and Evaluation: Top Ten Tools

Influence on Corporate Reputation	5.1	Crisis Mitigation	4.2
Influence on Employee Attitudes	4.8	Content Analysis of Clips	4.1
Metrics for Digital/Social	4.6	Influence on Share of Voice	4.0
Influence on Stakeholder Awareness	4.6	Total Impressions	4.0
Influence on Corporate Culture	4.5	Total Clips in Top-Tier Media	4.0

1=Don't use; 7=Use significantly

GAP | Generally Accepted Practices

USC Annenberg

Measurement and Evaluation: On the Rise

Measurement/Evaluation Approach	2009	2011	Increase
Metrics for Digital/Social	3.1	4.6	+1.5
Primary Research, Pre-Campaign	2.4	3.4	+1.0
Primary Research, Post-Campaign	2.6	3.5	+.9

1=Didn't use; 7=Used significantly

Growth is concentrated in more sophisticated, objective, quantitative techniques that are likely to provide strategic insight to guide campaigns and evaluate campaign outcomes.

GAP | Generally Accepted Practices

USC Annenberg

Measurement and Evaluation: Core *

Measurement/Eval Approach	GAP 2009	GAP 2011
Influence on Corporate Reputation	5.1	5.1
Influence on Employee Attitudes	4.4	4.8
Metrics for Digital/Social	3.1	4.6
Influence on Stakeholder Awareness	4.3	4.6
Influence on Corporate Culture	4.2	4.5
Crisis Mitigation	4.2	4.2
Content Analysis of Clips	4.6	4.1

*Above 4.0 average use

1=Didn't use; 7=Used significantly

Metrics of digital and social media have increased significantly since GAP VI. Another noticeable increase is its influence on employee attitudes and, to a lesser degree, on corporate culture. Content analysis of clips has declined.

Measurement and Evaluation: Categories (Factor Analysis)

USCAnnenberg

GAP | Generally Accepted Practices

Stakeholder outcomes	Strategic outcomes	PR outputs	Bottom line impact
Influence on corporate culture	Metrics for digital and social media	AVEs	Contribution to market share
Influence on corporate reputation	Primary research-pre-campaign	Content analysis of clips	Contribution to sales
Influence on employee attitudes	Primary research-post campaign	Clip counts	Influence on stock performance
Infl. on stakeholder awareness		Total circulation	
Crisis mitigation		Impressions	

*Factor analyses conducted using the full sample.

Factor analysis yielded four clusters indicating distinct categories of measurement. Outcomes measures (Stakeholder, Strategic and Bottom Line) are linked to indicators of success while PR outputs measures are not.

GAP VII, Section 5

Agency Relationships

USC Annenberg

GAP | Generally Accepted Practices

Agency Relationships: Fee Allocations as % of Total Budget

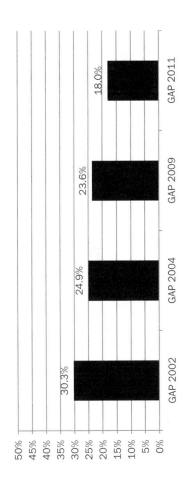

30.3%	24.9%	23.6%	18.0%
GAP 2002	GAP 2004	GAP 2009	GAP 2011

Corporations continue to allocate a smaller percentage of total budget to agencies. As the question wording changed from GAP VI to GAP VII, the most recent decline may be exaggerated. Also, as corporate communication/PR budgets have increased, the decline of actual agency budgets was modest.

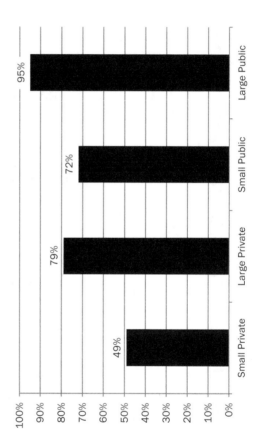

Agency Relationships: % Using Agencies

Small Private — 49%
Large Private — 79%
Small Public — 72%
Large Public — 95%

Use of agencies among large companies remains almost universal.

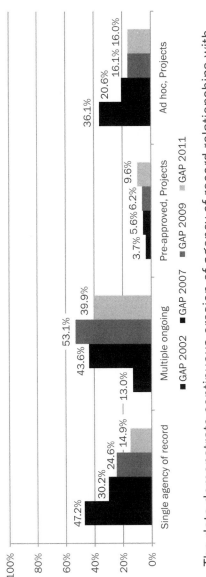

Agency Relationships: Type, Public Companies, 2002 - 2011

The data demonstrate continuous erosion of agency of record relationships with public companies. Four GAP studies show an undeniable trend: while in 2002 almost half of public companies worked with an agency of record, that number is down to 15% in 2011.

As shown previously, corporate clients tend towards working with several agencies simultaneously. For agencies, this is an unfortunate development as agency of record relationships tend to be durable and profitable.

193

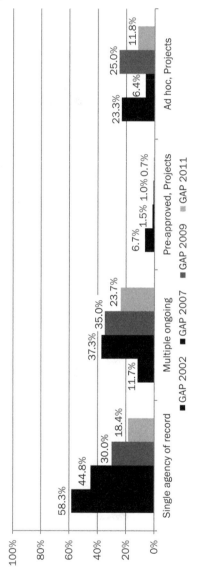

Agency Relationships: Type, Private Companies, 2002 - 2011

Single agency of record
- GAP 2002: 44.8%
- GAP 2007: 30.0%
- GAP 2009: 18.4%
- GAP 2011: 11.7%
- 58.3%

Multiple ongoing
- 37.3%
- 35.0%
- 23.7%

Pre-approved, Projects
- 6.7%
- 1.5% 1.0% 0.7%

Ad hoc, Projects
- 23.3%
- 25.0%
- 6.4%
- 11.8%

GAP 2002 ■ GAP 2007 ■ GAP 2009 ■ GAP 2011

There is also a clear trend among private companies away from agency-of-record relationships, down to less than 20%.

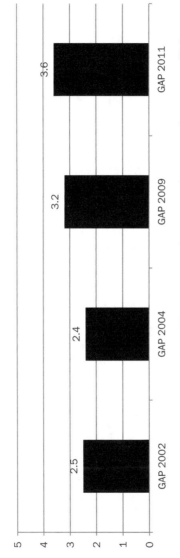

Number of Agencies Used, 2002 - 2011

The number of agencies retained by corporations continues to increase. This finding corresponds with the erosion of agency of record relationships and may be an indication of corporations' preferences to work with agencies specialized by function or geography.

GAP | Generally Accepted Practices

USC Annenberg

Agency Relationships: Reasons

Additional Arms and Legs	6.0	Help Quantify Results	4.4
Unique Perspective	5.7	Digital/Social Media	4.3
Marketing Insight	5.6	Limited Headcount	4.2
Strategic Point of View	5.3	Cheaper	4.1
Geographic Reach	4.5		

1=Not important; 7=Very important;
Among those reporting use of agencies.

All GAP studies including this one show "additional arms and legs" as the primary reason why corporations retain agencies. However, there agencies are also retained for strategic reasons, such as providing a unique perspective, marketing insight and providing a strategic point of view. Providing digital/social service ranks neutral in importance.

Only 18% indicate they have become more dependent on agencies for strategic insight in the last two years.

GAP | Generally Accepted Practices

USCAnnenberg

Agency Relationships: Strategic vs. Tactical (Factor Analysis)

Strategic	Tactical
Unique expertise	Cheaper than hiring staff
Market insights	For arms and legs
To quantify results	Because we have limited headcount
For their strategic point of view	

When looking into the motivations for corporate use of agencies, a factor analysis for all respondents reveals two clusters: strategic and tactical. Further analysis reveals a significant relationship between strategic agency use and (1) recommendations taken seriously, and (2) positive CEO perceptions.

Descriptively*, high strategic use, low tactical use, associated with strongest scores on multiple success factors. Descriptively, low strategic use, high tactical use, associated with weakest scores on multiple success factors (see typology on next slide).

*Small sample sizes within the typology do not permit tests of significance.

GAP | Generally Accepted Practices

USC Annenberg

Strategic vs. Tactical Agency Use by Corporations: a Typology

Strategic

	High	Low
Tactical High	High tactics, high strategy **27%**	High tactics, low strategy **17%**
Low	High strategy, low tactics **29%**	Low strategy, low tactics **26%**

GAP VII, Section 6

Organization/Reporting

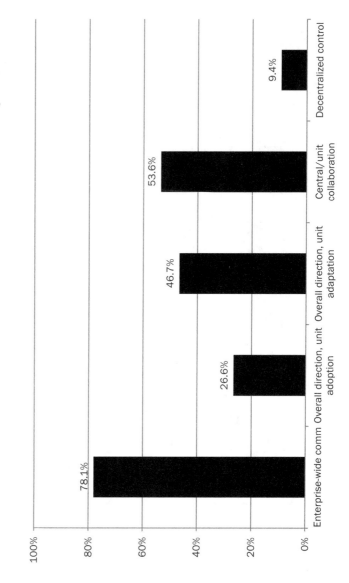

Degree of Central Control of Communication in Corporations

GAP | Generally
Accepted Practices

USC Annenberg

Reporting Line Analysis

Number of Reporting Lines in Corporations

The majority of corporate communication/PR departments (73%) have a single reporting line, whereas 27% report into multiple functions.

Among those with multiple reporting lines, 51% report to marketing and a member of the C-suite. 33% report to human resources and a member of the C-suite.

Private companies have a higher level of multiple reports (33%) than public (23%).

Satisfaction with Reporting Lines in Corporations

When asked if corporate respondents thought their current reporting line is appropriate, 60% strongly agreed while 16% strongly disagreed. It is noteworthy that there was no difference in the perceived effectiveness between single (5.20 on 7-point scale) and multiple reports (5.24).

The reason for this is that a large majority (88%) of multiple reports have a line to the C-Suite compared to only 44% of single reports. Overall, those with C-suite access are more satisfied (5.87) than those without (4.33).

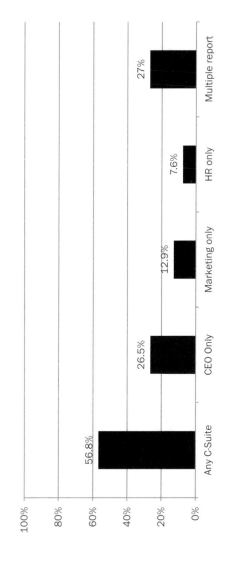

Reporting Lines - Corporate Respondents

Among corporations, the reporting lines of PR/Comm is consistent with past GAP studies.

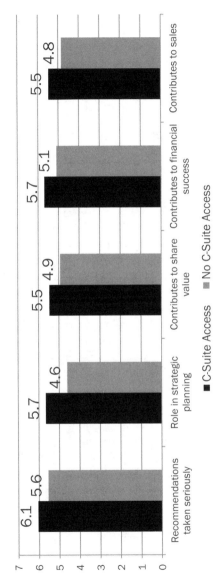

Reporting Lines and Perceived Value of PR Among Corporations

Corporate PR/Comm departments with C-suite access are consistently perceived to be of higher value to their companies than those without C-suite access.

GAP | Generally Accepted Practices

USC Annenberg

Relationship between Reporting lines and Integration among Corporations

Integration, for the purpose of the GAP studies, measures coordination of communication activities within the PR/Comm function (intra-departmental integration), and whether PR/Comm programs are aligned and coordinated with activities of other corporate functions (inter-departmental integration). In GAP VII, analysis shows that both intra-departmental and inter-departmental integrations are powerful contributors to success.

When corporate PR/Comm departments have a direct line into the C-suite, they report a higher level of intra-departmental integration (5.5 of 7) than if they do not (5.1). The same finding applies to inter-departmental integration: 5.5 with C-suite access, 4.9 without. Data further show a strong relationship between C-suite access and getting invited to strategy meetings (5.7 vs. 4.6).

A reporting line may sometimes be situational (i.e. marketing-driven companies), but broader conclusions are inescapable. To achieve its full potential, corporate communication/PR must be included in the Dominant Coalition, i.e. report to the C-suite. Reasons for non-inclusion would be organizational and/or professional limitations.

GAP VII, Section 7

C-Suite Perceptions

USC Annenberg

GAP | Generally Accepted Practices

C-Suite Perceptions: The Role of PR/Comm

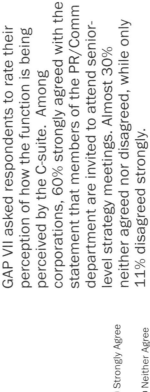

GAP VII asked respondents to rate their perception of how the function is being perceived by the C-suite. Among corporations, 60% strongly agreed with the statement that members of the PR/Comm department are invited to attend senior-level strategy meetings. Almost 30% neither agreed nor disagreed, while only 11% disagreed strongly.

Measured on a 7-point scale. 'Strongly agree' equals 6/7. 'Strongly disagree' equals 1/2.

■ Strongly Agree

■ Neither Agree nor Disagree

■ Strongly Disagree

59.7%

29.2%

11.0%

PR/Communications Attends Senior-Level Strategic Planning Meetings

100%

80%

60%

40%

20%

0%

C-Suite Perceptions: The Role of PR/COM

The same pattern prevailed when corporate respondents were asked whether they perceive their recommendations as being taken seriously. In fact, only 4.4% strongly disagreed.

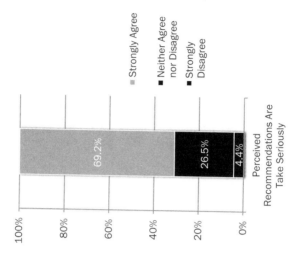

Perceived Recommendations Are Take Seriously

- Strongly Agree
- Neither Agree nor Disagree
- Strongly Disagree

69.2%
26.5%
4.4%

Measured on a 7-point scale. 'Strongly agree' equals 6/7. 'Strongly disagree' equals 1/2.

GAP | Generally Accepted Practices

USC Annenberg

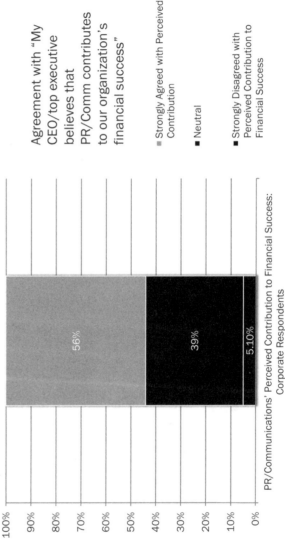

C-Suite Perceptions: Contributions to Financial Success

Agreement with "My CEO/top executive believes that PR/Comm contributes to our organization's financial success"

- Strongly Agreed with Perceived Contribution
- Neutral
- Strongly Disagreed with Perceived Contribution to Financial Success

56%

39%

5.10%

PR/Communications' Perceived Contribution to Financial Success: Corporate Respondents

Measured on a 7-point scale. 'Strongly agree' equals 6/7. 'Strongly disagree' equals 1/2.

100%
90%
80%
70%
60%
50%
40%
30%
20%
10%
0%

GAP | Generally Accepted Practices

USCAnnenberg

GAP VII, Section 8

Organizational Integration

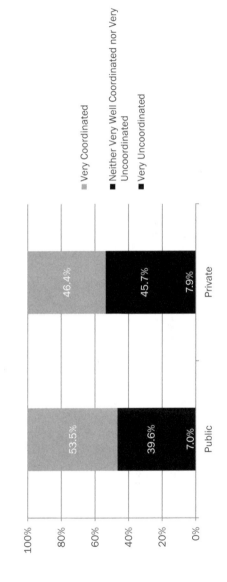

Intra-Functional Integration Among Communication Functions

GAP | Generally Accepted Practices

USC Annenberg

Over 50% of corporate respondents, both public and private, report a very high level of coordination within the function, while well below 10% say the PR/Comm function is very uncoordinated.

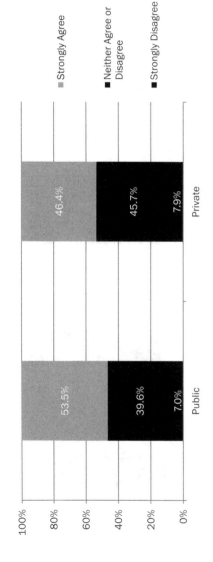

Organizational Integration: Inter-Functional Integration Among Corporate Respondents

When it comes to inter-functional integration of PR/Comm with other departments such as finance, legal, operations, etc., more respondents in public companies (53.3%) say they feel very well integrated, while that number drops to 46.6% among private company respondents. For both categories, less than 10% report a low level of integration.

211

USC Annenberg

GAP | Generally Accepted Practices

Intra-Departmental Integration Equals Success (Corporate Respondents)

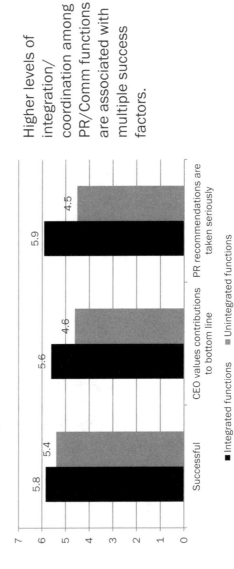

Higher levels of integration/ coordination among PR/Comm functions are associated with multiple success factors.

Coordinated functions is defined as a score above 4.0 on a 1- 7 scale; CEO values contributions=average agreement with "My CEO/top exec. believes PR contributes to... stock valuation, financial success, sales; PR recommendations= average agreement with "PR recs taken seriously..." and "PR generally invited to senior-level meetings..."

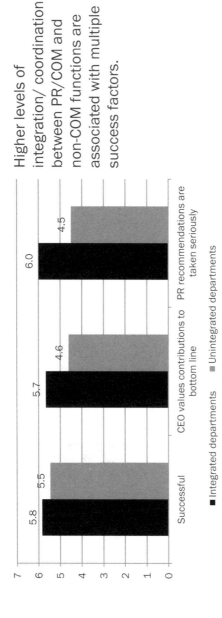

Inter-Departmental Integration Equals Success (Corporate Respondents)

GAP Generally Accepted Practices

USCAnnenberg

Higher levels of integration/ coordination between PR/COM and non-COM functions are associated with multiple success factors.

Coordinated departments is defined as a score above 4.0 on a 1- 7 scale; CEO values contributions=average agreement with "My CEO/top exec. believes PR contributes to... stock valuation, financial success, sales; PR recommendations=average agreement with "PR recs taken seriously..." and "PR generally invited to senior-level meetings..."

■ Integrated departments ■ Unintegrated departments

Successful | CEO values contributions to bottom line | PR recommendations are taken seriously

5.8 | 5.5 | 5.7 | 4.6 | 6.0 | 4.5

A Culture of Integration

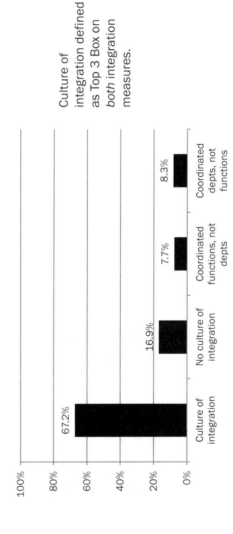

Culture of integration defined as Top 3 Box on *both* integration measures.

Culture of integration	67.2%
No culture of integration	16.9%
Coordinated functions, not depts	7.7%
Coordinated depts, not functions	8.3%

Types of integration are highly correlated (r=.68); nearly 70% of corporations report both kinds of integration; 17% are not integrated at all.

USCAnnenberg

GAP | Generally Accepted Practices

Culture of Integration: All Respondents

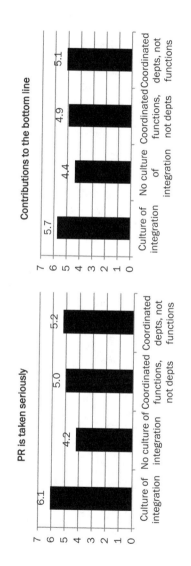

PR is taken seriously

Culture of integration	6.1
No culture of integration	4.2
Coordinated functions, not depts	5.0
Coordinated depts, not functions	5.2

Contributions to the bottom line

Culture of integration	5.7
No culture of integration	4.4
Coordinated functions, not depts	4.9
Coordinated depts, not functions	5.1

Organizations with a culture of integration are significantly more likely than any others to report that PR/Comm is highly valued.

Significant multiple comparison tests with Bonferroni correction.

GAP VII, Section 9

Excellence and Best Practices

GAP | Generally Accepted Practices

USCAnnenberg

Excellence and Best Practices – Key Insights for Success

The GAP VII findings confirm a set of best practices that were identified in previous GAP studies and are all strongly associated with success variables. Patterns are very compelling and long-lived over multiple GAP studies.

Integration: Champion intra-functional and inter-functional integration and coordination

Measurement/Evaluation: Invest at least the average percentage (9%) of total budget in measurement and evaluation; focus investment on metrics other than media outputs.

Culture/Character: Beginning within the PR/Comm function, champion the adoption of a culture or character that is proactive, long-term, strategic, flexible, ethical, and people-first.

Agency Relationships: Optimize strategic value over mainly tactical use.

Reporting Line: Assure that PR/Comm has the most effective reporting line, given the nature and structure of the entire organization. In most cases this will be a direct reporting line to the C-Suite. Be part of the Dominant Coalition.

GAP | Generally Accepted Practices

USC Annenberg

Excellence and Best Practices, Key Insight: A Period of Profound Transition from Old School to New School

GAP VII findings indicate an industry in transition from 'old school' to 'new school' approaches to managing the PR/Comm function. Companies that embrace 'new school' best practices are more likely to be associated with success variables.

Old School

- Measurement of media outputs
- Believe PR focus is on media relations
- Does not believe social media are pervasive
- Reactive/Short-term
- Worried about control
- Consider media relations the dominating discipline of PR

New School

- Measurement of outcomes
- Assign primary responsibility for social media to PR
- Long-term strategic direction
- Embrace multiplying touchpoints, pervasiveness of social media – still with modicum of control
- More likely to believe recommendations are taken seriously

Index